RAYMOND E. BROWN, S.S.

READING *the* GOSPELS
With *the* CHURCH

From Christmas Through Easter

WIPF & STOCK · Eugene, Oregon

Wipf and Stock Publishers
199 W 8th Ave, Suite 3
Eugene, OR 97401

Reading the Gospels With the Church
From Christmas Through Easter
By Brown, Raymond E.
Copyright©1996 by Brown, Raymond E.
ISBN 13: 978-1-55635-963-7
Publication date 12/17/2008
Previously published by St. Anthony Messenger Press, 1996

Contents

To ROLAND E. MURPHY, O. CARM.,
long-time friend and coworker in interpreting the Scriptures,
in celebration of his eightieth birthday (July 1997).
No one has done more to make Old Testament Wisdom
living wisdom for believers today.

Introduction

What is the best way to familiarize people with the Bible? Having discovered the marvelous wealth of the Bible from reading by myself, not through courses in school, I am convinced that with a little effort people can become fascinated by the Scriptures. But something needs to get them started. The incentive probably differs for different people. Yet one that has served many well is the liturgy—the weekly reading of Bible passages in Church services.

That is particularly true of the Gospel readings in the seasons dedicated to the great events in the life of Christ: Christmas, Lent, Holy Week and Easter. Reflections on the Gospels of those seasons can constitute a wonderful entry into appreciating the Bible. That is what I mean by entitling this book *Reading the Gospels With the Church*.

Over the years, in an attempt to facilitate this approach, I have written *Catholic Updates*—those splendidly practical, short, inexpensive publications designed for parish consumption. Yet the very format that makes them so useful—a folded sheet with four printed sides—tends to make them disposable rather than permanent.

Some who have liked my *Updates* have suggested that they be gathered into a book. This seemed like a good idea, provided that I could add some material. Accordingly, almost half this book has not appeared in *Updates* (Chapters One, Two, Six and the Appendix), although I have striven to phrase that new material in the popular *Update* style. I believe that the end product is cohesive and useful on a larger scale. It is my fondest hope that those who pick up this book will understand better the Gospels read in the liturgy and come to see how reflection on the Bible might enrich their lives.

Although I am a Roman Catholic priest and know Catholic audiences best, I have worked a good deal of my life with Protestant clergy. One of God's graces in our times is that the mainline Churches now read much the same Scripture on Sundays. Therefore there is no reason why this book could not be useful to Protestant and Anglican audiences as well. The Appendix, which is a short excerpt from a Roman Catholic Church document, also may be interesting to them, so that they can see what a common stance is now shared by that Church and their own.

Raymond E. Brown, S.S.

CHAPTER ONE

The Church and the Bible: A New Understanding

Very often when older Catholics hear at Mass a presentation about the Bible they are puzzled. In their youth they were probably never encouraged to read the Bible, and what is now being said about biblical stories (for instance, about Adam and Eve) bears little resemblance to what they heard when they were growing up. A similar confusion sometimes occurs when youngsters come home and report to their parents what they were taught about the Bible in religion class. The parents wonder whether this can be correct.

A simple answer to part of the confusion is that in the mid-twentieth century the Catholic Church drastically changed its position on the Scriptures. It did so because it saw how new methods greatly increased the understanding of the Bible and made its wealth more accessible and spiritually helpful. A brief survey of the history of the change will give readers background for the chapters to follow in this book.

The End of the Nineteenth Century

Our story begins in the last quarter of the nineteenth century, which was a very active period in the study of the Bible. The movement to submit the scriptural books to the same kind of historical and literary analysis as other ancient literature had been gaining force in Protestant circles, especially in Germany. It was now leading to solutions startlingly different from those held in the tradition. For instance, the Pentateuchal section of the Old Testament (the first five books) had been attributed to Moses by both Christians and Jews. In the 1870's and 1880's, however, a famous scholar, Julius Wellhausen, argued that these books were composed from four documents written four to eight hundred years after Moses.

Discoveries of Assyrian, Babylonian and Egyptian writings suggested that some biblical stories (like that of the flood), law codes and collections of wisdom had been borrowed from other nations. Anglican scholars, recognizing that the King James translation of the New Testament had been based on an inferior Greek manuscript tradition, used ancient manuscripts to print a superior Greek version on which new English translations were subsequently based.

We are accustomed today to receive encyclicals from the pope or directives from Vatican offices on controverted questions. But that was not always so. This ferment about new biblical methods and discoveries brought the papacy for the first time directly into Catholic discussions of the Bible with the encyclical *Providentissimus Deus* of Pope Leo XIII (1893).

Personally a very learned man, the pope recognized the value of some scholarly advances and spoke with considerable nuance about the situation. Nevertheless, he insisted on the Latin version (not the original Greek or Hebrew) as a basis of translation and on the traditional interpretations of scriptural passages. Happily, his encyclical spared Catholics a problem that would trouble many pious Protestants in relation to human evolution. It pointed out that the biblical authors, who shared the "scientific" views of their times, do not teach answers to problems raised by the natural sciences of our times.

The First Third of the Twentieth Century

On the academic scene, the turn of the century and the early 1900's saw among scholars an even more rapid acceptance of modern approaches to the Bible, often with a radical twist. Many scholars were saying that the Bible was not simply a history. For some, that meant calling into doubt the truth of important biblical affirmations like God's creation of the world, miracles, the divinity of Jesus, the Incarnation and the Resurrection, and so on. Recognizing that the Judeo-Christian faith was being undermined, conservative Protestants in the United States banded together to protect "the fundamentals" by insisting on the literal historicity of everything described in the Scriptures—whence the name "Fundamentalism" (see Chapter Eight).

About the same time (more precisely, between 1905 and 1915), fearing that the radical Protestant scholarship would make its way into Catholic circles, the Roman Pontifical Biblical Commission issued a series of cautionary, conservative decrees rejecting most of the positions taken by contemporary Protestant academics. The Commission affirmed that Moses was substantially the author of the Pentateuch; Isaiah was one book; essentially, Matthew wrote the first Gospel and the apostle John the fourth; Paul wrote the Letters to Timothy and Titus. In the 1920's the Vatican Holy Office took vigorous action against any Catholic deviations from traditional positions on the Bible. These directives shaped textbooks and classroom teaching for decades to come (and that means what many of us were taught in classes dealing with Bible stories in Catholic grammar schools).

Thus, for the first third of the twentieth century one may speak of three trends in biblical interpretation. At most major Protestant divinity schools (universities and seminaries) the professors, recognizing the very real problems detected by modern historical and literary methods, advocated an approach that called into question the traditional authorship of the biblical books and recognized that many of them were far from exact histories of what they described. In reaction, fundamentalist and evangelist preachers and Bible colleges, in varying ways, contradicted such an approach by insisting on the literal inerrancy of the Scriptures. Catholics, a third and isolated group ignored by both Protestant camps, held onto the traditional Christian doctrines by absolute fidelity to the positions inculcated by the Pontifical Biblical Commission.

The Period of Change: 1940-1965

Suddenly, in the 1940's during the pontificate of Pope Pius XII, the Catholic position changed. Here was a pope whose personal experience showed how wonderfully enriching Bible reading could be for the spiritual life. Change was now opportune because the mainstream of scholarly Protestant research had shifted back toward the center, as radical positions were challenged by recent discoveries. For instance, the view that John's Gospel was written about A.D. 175 had been shown untenable by the dating of a small papyrus fragment of that Gospel to about 135, so that the traditional assignment of the composition of the Gospel to the 90's again became likely. Clay tablets discovered at Ugarit in Syria revealed a Canaanite language akin to Hebrew and suggested to scholars that some Old Testament poetry should be dated before 1000 B.C., thus contradicting the late dating proposed by Wellhausen.

Consequently, in his encyclical *Divino Afflante Spiritu* (1943), Pius XII judged that it was safe for Catholic scholars to take up the methods that were previously forbidden. Translations from the original Hebrew and Greek were now encouraged. A particular aspect of the encyclical definitively steered Catholics away from fundamentalism: namely, the recognition that the Bible includes many different literary forms or genres, not just history. One might exemplify this by thinking of the Bible as the library both of ancient Israel and of the early Church, containing different kinds of history, poetry, drama, dramatized parables and so on. It is a bad mistake to wander into a modern library, pick up a historical novel or a play and read it as if it were exact history—the kind of mistake that literalists tend to make in dealing with the biblical books.

After the end of the Second World War, *Divino Afflante Spiritu* sparked an enormous growth in Catholic biblical scholarship. New teachers were trained, and the results of the changed approach to the Scriptures were gradually communicated to the people—the very steps the pope had urged. A statement of the Pontifical Biblical Commission to Cardinal Suhard of Paris in 1948 documented a change in Church attitudes toward the Pentateuch. Rather than being composed at one time by Moses, these first Old Testament books were composed from sources and developed in the course of history. While the early chapters of Genesis (including the Adam and Eve story) relate fundamental truths, they do so in figurative language and do not contain history in a modern sense.

By 1955 the secretary of the Pontifical Biblical Commission could declare that now Catholic scholars had complete liberty with regard to the 1905-1915 decrees of that Commission except where they touched on faith and morals (and very few of them did). This meant that Catholic scholars were free to adopt positions of authorship and dating that other Christians had come to hold under the pressure of evidence.

A crucial moment occurred at the beginning of the Second Vatican Council in 1962. Pius XII had died, and it soon became evident that not everyone in Rome approved of the biblical changes he had introduced. The preliminary document on the sources of revelation, sent out by the Holy Office before the Council as a basis for discussion, appealed to positions taken in the early 1900's and would have turned the clock back. This document was rejected by nearly two-thirds of the Council participants and sent back by Pope John XXIII for thorough rewriting.

As part of the rewriting, the important "The Historical Truth of the Gospels"—*Instruction* of the Roman Pontifical Biblical Commission (1964) became the basis of the final Vatican II document pertinent to Scripture (*Dogmatic Constitution on Divine Revelation*, promulgated in 1965). (Chapter Two below will draw heavily on this *Instruction* and its teaching about three stages of Gospel formation.) The Commission held that the Gospels, while retaining the sense of the sayings of Jesus, were not necessarily expressing them literally. The truth and historicity of the Gospels must be judged from the fact that the doctrine and life of Jesus were not reported for the purpose of being remembered but were preached so as to offer the Church a basis of faith and morals.

This Biblical Commission approach, which steers Catholics away from a literalist approach to the Gospels, was fortified by Vatican II's position on inerrancy: "The books of Scripture must be acknowledged as teaching firmly, faithfully, and without error that truth which God wanted put into the sacred writings for the sake of our salvation" (*Divine Revelation*, 11). That is a far cry from assuming that every statement in Scripture has to be literally accurate.

From 1965 Till Today: Consolidation and New Problems

In the last third of the century, since the end of the Second Vatican Council, Church needs have shaped developments in the Catholic approach to the Bible. A new set of liturgical books provided three years of Sunday Mass readings, involving not only the Old Testament (a most important innovation), but almost the complete texts of Mark, Matthew and Luke (one for each year; John is read every year, mostly in the Lenten and Easter seasons). As we shall see in the next chapter, that method of not mixing passages from one Gospel with those from another reflects the view that each evangelist had his own theology and viewpoint that guided not only what he narrated but how he did so. For liturgical purposes, translations from the original languages were made into the vernacular languages of the world—translations done according to modern standards of scholarship.

The Vatican Council had encouraged ecumenical relations, and Catholic and Protestant biblical specialists started to work together on some of these translations, as well as on sensitive issues that divided the Churches (like the biblical presentation of Peter and of Mary). Academics from the different confessions began to teach on the others' university and seminary faculties, for Catholic biblical scholarship and middle-of-the-road Protestant scholarship could agree on the meaning of much of the Scriptures. Within a remarkably short time Catholic scholarly production had reached equality in the eyes of all.

Where are we today? Inevitably, there are both encouraging and discouraging factors. Fortunately, Catholic biblical scholarship has remained remarkably untroubled in its relationship to Church authority, and directives from Rome have remained positive. The decline in the number of Catholic clergy means that in the foreseeable future lay biblical scholars will become a majority on the Catholic scene. That can be very helpful in terms of new endeavor and perspective, but some of them will not have the general background in theology and Church history given to priests in the seminary. There may be difficulties in combining the scientific and the pastoral aspects of scriptural presentation.

The general biblical scene is complicated. The historical analysis so prominent at the beginning of the nineteenth century has remained important, but new methods of analysis have come into prominence. Indeed, in 1993 the Pontifical Biblical Commission produced a document stressing how these approaches could be complementary—a salutary reaction to a tendency to make one or the other the only important way to read Scripture.

New discoveries have also produced mixed benefits. The Dead Sea Scrolls, uncovered in Palestine beginning in 1947, are very helpful in supplying information on the text of the Hebrew Bible, on noncanonical biblical books and on the theology of a group of Jews who flourished from the second century B.C. to the first century A.D. The delay in publishing some fragments, however, has fueled bizarre conspiracy theories about the suppression of damaging facts and fantastic claims that Christian leaders are described figuratively in the scrolls.

In 1945 a library of Coptic documents stemming from the fourth century A.D. was discovered in Egypt. Many of them exhibit a Gnostic vein of thought regarded as heretical by the Church Fathers. Some were translated from earlier Greek originals, and a number of radical scholars would exalt them as more original than our canonical New Testament.

Radio and TV often complicate a balanced approach to such issues. On the one hand, particularly in the southern and southwestern United States, fundamentalist and literalist preachers occupy a good deal of media time defending the word-for-word historicity of the Bible and issuing predictions based on the misunderstanding that Daniel and Revelation are exact prophecies of the future. They reject much modern Catholic and centrist Protestant exegesis.

On the other hand, hypotheses based on little evidence (such as some of those promoted by the "Jesus Seminar") propose extravagant reinterpretations of Christian origins and are presented in the media as the latest scholarship. It is difficult to find on the radio or TV a presentation of the centrist approach to Scripture, which is actually the most commonly taught and held. Fortunately, a good number of books, Catholic and Protestant, embody that approach.

Perhaps the most encouraging element in the present Catholic picture is the number of people interested in the Bible. One hundred years ago it was almost axiomatic that Catholics did not read the Bible; the twentieth century has changed that picture dramatically.

CHAPTER TWO

How to Understand the Gospels

Having surveyed the general change in the Catholic Church's attitude toward biblical study, let us now turn to the sensitive area of the Gospels. I have often thought that in January, as we begin in parishes to read the Gospel for the Sundays of a new year (Matthew for Year A; Mark for Year B; Luke for Year C), it would be helpful for priests to devote a homily to what a Gospel is, and another homily to what is special about the Gospel that will be read all year long.

Many people probably think of the Gospels as biographies of Jesus. They are not. As we shall see in Chapter Three, some of the most basic biographical information about Jesus (when and where born, name of a parent) is absent from Mark and from John. Even more people would be unaware of how much one Gospel differs from another. The sharp differences not only raise further difficulties for the biographical approach (and perhaps create fears about the historical truth of the Gospels) but also lead into the question of the origin and goal of the Gospels.

The Three Stages of Gospel Formation

Fortunately, the Church has given us a very helpful guide for dealing with these issues—a guide that wins the approval of most centrist scholars and exemplifies the harmonious relationship between Church authority and Catholic scholarship described in Chapter One. I refer to the *Instruction* on "The Historical Truth of the Gospels," issued by the

Roman Pontifical Biblical Commission in 1964 (the substance of which was incorporated into Vatican II's *Constitution on Divine Revelation* in 1965).

When some Catholics are told that the Gospels are not necessarily literal accounts of the ministry of Jesus, they become suspicious of the "orthodoxy" of the person who makes such a claim. It may be important, therefore, to stress that this *Instruction*, which offers that evaluation, constitutes a teaching of the Catholic Church binding on all its members. I plan to use the *Instruction* as a springboard to explain the Gospels, and shall elaborate its implications. Since many readers may find it useful to have the actual text, it is included as an Appendix to this book on page 87. No better guidance can be offered in Bible discussion groups or catechetical teaching.

The *Instruction* begins its treatment of the reliability of the Gospels by insisting that diligent attention should be paid to *the three stages of tradition* by which the life and teaching of Jesus have come down to us. Those three stages, which follow chronologically one upon the other, are: (1) the ministry of Jesus, (2) the preaching of the apostles and (3) the writing by the evangelists. We would not be far off from common scholarly opinion if we assigned one third of the first century A.D. to each, since Jesus died about 30-33, the main preaching apostles were dead by the mid-60's and the evangelists probably wrote in the period 65-100.

Stage One: The Public Ministry of Jesus of Nazareth

We may date this stage to the first third of the first century A.D. The *Instruction* does not concern itself with Jesus' birth and infancy (see Chapter Three below). (In fact, several years after the *Instruction* was issued, the Roman Pontifical Commission did meet to discuss the historicity of the Infancy narratives, presumably with the hope of issuing a similar instruction pertinent to them—a project never completed.) Rather, the *Instruction* focuses on the words and deeds of Jesus from the time of his calling the first disciples.

Jesus did noteworthy things (which the first three Gospels label "deeds of power" and we refer to as miracles) as he orally proclaimed his message. At the same time, he chose companions who traveled with him, who saw and heard what he said and did. Their memories of his words and deeds supplied the raw Jesus material or Jesus tradition that would be preached in Stage Two. These memories were already selective since they concentrated on what pertained to Jesus' proclamation of God, not the many details of ordinary existence—some of which would have been included if a biography were intended.

On a practical level it is important for modern readers to keep reminding themselves that these were memories of what was said and done by a Jew who lived in Galilee, Jerusalem and environs in the 20's. Jesus' manner of speaking, the problems he faced, his vocabulary and outlook were those of that specific time, place and circumstance. Often he had new ways of looking at things, but his newness did not remove him from his time and place. Many failures to understand Jesus and misapplications of his thoughts stem from the fact that people who read the Gospels do remove him from space and time and imagine that Jesus was dealing with issues he never encountered.

Both liberal and conservative Christians make that mistake. For instance, liberal pacifist Christians may ask whether Jesus would serve as a soldier in a modern war (in Vietnam or in the Gulf). The exact if somewhat brutal answer to such a question is that a Galilean Jew would not have known of the existence of Vietnam or of mechanized war. A better phrased question would be: In fidelity to what Jesus taught and to his example, what is a *Christian's* duty in relation to a modern war?

Conservative Christians often want to settle questions of Church structure and practice by appealing to Jesus. Once, after a series of lectures on the origin of the Church, a well-intentioned member of the audience asked me: "Why didn't Jesus prevent all future confusion by saying, 'I came to found the Roman Catholic Church; the Bishop of Rome, the pope, will be the leader of the Church, and everyone must obey him'?" The difficulty is that Jesus is recorded as having spoken of *church* only twice in all the Gospels (Matthew 16:18; 18:17; in the latter he is clearly talking about a local community). Thus there is little recorded proof that he spent much time thinking about the structure of a future Church. Rather, he was concerned with proclaiming God's Kingdom or rule to those whom he encountered in his lifetime.

Moreover, a Galilean Jew would scarcely have thought of an institution in Rome, where the emperor was, or of categories like pope and bishop. A better phrasing of the issue is whether the community called Church that emerged from the preaching of Jesus' followers and the centralizing of that Church in Rome where Peter died as a martyr are valid developments from what he proclaimed, and whether, in that sense, that Church may be said to be founded by him.

We Catholics answer yes, for we trace *a line of development* from what Jesus said and did to what the apostles said and did, and to later growth. In Christian faith the Jesus tradition truly has decisive ramifications for problems and issues that did not appear in his lifetime. *The Holy Spirit* clarifies these ramifications by helping to translate from Jesus' time to subsequent periods. Church life and teaching are the usual context of such translation. That is why, when we meet together to worship on Sunday, the Gospels are not simply read but also preached on so as to bring out their implications for our time. When Church documents speak about the actions of "Christ" or "Jesus Christ," they are not simply talking about Jesus as he was in his public ministry but also about the Jesus portrayed in apostolic preaching and reflected on in subsequent tradition and development.

Stage Two: The Apostolic Preaching About Jesus

We may date this to the second third of the first century A.D. The Biblical Commission *Instruction* says: "After Jesus rose from the dead and his divinity was clearly perceived"—a recognition by the Church that during the ministry of Jesus, although his disciples followed him, they did not fully perceive who he was. In this stage, then, a whole new perception colors the Jesus tradition.

Appearances of the risen Jesus confirmed what his followers had seen and heard during his public ministry (1 Corinthians 15:5-7) and brought them to full faith in him as the one through whom God had effected salvation for Israel and eventually the whole world. They vocalized this faith through the titles under which we find Jesus confessed (Messiah/Christ, Lord, Savior, Son of God and so on), all of which were gradually transformed by the perception of his divinity. Such postresurrectional faith illumined the memories of what the disciples had seen and heard before the Resurrection, and so they proclaimed his words and deeds with enriched significance. This was not a distortion of the Jesus tradition from Stage One; rather, it involved a perception of what was already there but had not previously been recognized. (Modern readers, accustomed to a media goal of uninvolved, factual reporting, need to understand that this was not at all the atmosphere of early Christian preaching, which was committed and interpretative.)

We speak of these preachers as "apostolic" because they understood themselves as sent forth (*apostellein*) by the risen Jesus, and their preaching is often described as kerygmatic proclamation (*kerygma*) intended to bring others to faith. Eventually the circle of missionary preachers was enlarged beyond the original companions of Jesus, and the faith experiences of all the preachers enriched what they had received and were now proclaiming.

Another factor operative in this stage of development was the necessary adaptation of the preaching to a new audience. If Jesus was a Galilean Jew of the first third of the first century, by mid-century the gospel was being preached in cities to urban Jews and Gentiles in Greek, a language that Jesus did not normally speak (if he spoke it at all or knew more than a few phrases). This change of language involved translation in the broadest sense of that term, that is, a rephrasing of the message in vocabulary and patterns that would make it intelligible and alive for new audiences. The *Instruction* speaks of the various "literary forms" into which the Jesus tradition was shaped, forms that "were accustomed to be used by the people of that time."

In terms of vocabulary, sometimes the rephrasing affected incidentals. For instance, Luke 5:19 substitutes a tile roof familiar to a Greek audience for the Palestinian village-style roof of pressed clay and branches through which a hole was opened (Mark 2:4). But other choices had theological repercussions. For instance, Jesus spoke in Aramaic at the Last Supper of his "flesh and blood." The more literal Greek translation, *sarx*, "flesh," is attested in John 6:51 and Ignatius of Antioch's *Epistle to the Romans* 7:3, and so on, but the first three Gospels and 1 Corinthians 11:24 chose an idiomatic Greek translation, *soma*, "body," for the eucharistic component. That choice may have facilitated the figurative use of *body* in the theology of the Body of Christ of which Christians are members (1 Corinthians 12:12-27). Thus developments in this preaching period of the Jesus tradition served the growth of Christian theology.

Another type of development came from encountering new issues that Jesus never dealt with. The first three Gospels and Paul agree that Jesus took a severe stance against divorce and remarriage: If a man divorces his wife and marries another, he commits adultery. But Jesus was dealing with Jews. How was his demand to be applied once Christianity began to be preached among the Gentiles? Jewish women could not divorce Jewish men, but in many Gentile areas women could divorce men. Mark 10:12 (and Mark alone) has a second demand: If a woman divorces her husband and marries another, she commits adultery. Jesus probably never said that, but it was the obvious corollary of his teaching as the preachers encountered this new possibility.

Similarly, Matthew 5:32; 19:9 (and Matthew alone) adds an exceptive phrase: If a man divorces his wife, except for *porneia*, and marries another, he commits adultery. On the basis of other New Testament uses (1 Corinthians 5:1; Acts 15:20), it seems likely that by *porneia* Matthew means unions within the forbidden degrees of kindred—"forbidden" and deemed impure by the Mosaic Law and therefore not encountered among Jews, but encountered by the preachers among Gentiles. Matthew is teaching that a man not only can but should divorce a wife who is close kinfolk because that is no marriage at all.

We may find it odd that such expansions (or "explications," to use the language of section IX of the *Instruction*) are included *within* the words of Jesus. If we were writing the account, we would have Jesus' words in the body of the text and add explanatory footnotes in order to apply his teaching to situations unforeseen by him. But one cannot preach with footnotes, and both original word and explication became part of the preached Jesus tradition.

Paul, writing letters, could be more precise. In 1 Corinthians 7:10-11 he presents as a word of the Lord that a man should not divorce his wife and that any woman separated from her husband cannot remarry. But then a few verses later (7:12-15) he deals with a situation that Jesus never dealt with by a word of his own, which he stresses is *not* a word of the Lord. In the case of a believing Christian married to a nonbeliever, if they cannot live together in peace and the unbelieving partner desires to separate, let it be so. Had Paul been writing a Gospel, such an exception might very well have found its way into the text describing Jesus' attitude toward marriage!

I hope these examples help to show how remarkably formative was this Stage Two of Gospel development. While staying substantially faithful to "what was really said and done by Jesus" and in that sense remaining historical, it moved away from exact, literal retention and reproduction, and thus kept the Jesus tradition alive, meaningful and salvific, even as it was in Stage One when it originated.

Stage Three: The Written Gospels

We may date this stage to the last third of the first century A.D. Although in the middle of the previous period, as the

Jesus tradition was being preached, some early written collections (now lost) would have appeared, and although preaching based on *oral* preservation and development of the Jesus tradition continued well into the second century, the era from 65 to 100 was probably when all four canonical Gospels were written.

According to titles ("The Gospel according to ...") attached in the late second century, two Gospels were attributed to the eyewitness apostles Matthew and John and two to "apostolic men" who themselves were not eyewitnesses: Mark, the companion of Peter, and Luke, the companion of Paul. Yet relatively few modern scholars think that any evangelist was an eyewitness of the ministry of Jesus. This surely represents a change of view. Yet the shift may not be so sharp as first seems, for it is not clear that the early traditions about authors were always referring to the writer in our sense of the one who put the Gospel on papyrus. Ancient attribution may have been concerned with the one responsible for the tradition enshrined in a particular Gospel, the *author*ity behind the Gospel, or the one who wrote one of the main sources of the Gospel. The section of the *Instruction* of the Biblical Commission that treats Stage Three does not deal with this question directly. But the *Instruction* takes care to speak of "apostles" in Stage Two and of "sacred authors/writers" in Stage Three, as if two different sets of people were involved.

The wide recognition that the evangelists were *not* eyewitnesses of Jesus' ministry is important for understanding the differences among the Gospels. In the older approach wherein eyewitness testimony was directly involved, it was very difficult to explain differences among the Gospels. How could eyewitness John report the cleansing of the temple at the beginning of the ministry (2:13-17) and eyewitness Matthew report it at the end (21:12-13)? To reconcile them it was maintained that the cleansing of the temple happened twice and that each evangelist chose to report only one instance.

Many other examples of improbable reconciliations

stemming from the theory of direct eyewitness accuracy can be offered. Since Matthew has a Sermon on the Mount and Luke has a similar Sermon on the Plain (Matthew 5:1; Luke 6:17), there must have been a plain on the side of the mountain! Since Matthew has the Lord's Prayer taught in that sermon and Luke has it later on the road to Jerusalem (Matthew 6:9-13; Luke 11:2-4), the disciples must have forgotten it, so that Jesus repeated it! Mark places the healing of the blind man after Jesus left Jericho (10:46); Luke places it before Jesus entered Jericho (18:35; 19:1). Perhaps Jesus was leaving the site of Old Testament Jericho and entering the site of New Testament Jericho!

On the other hand, if direct eyewitness writing was not involved, these harmonizing improbabilities can be avoided. Each evangelist was the recipient of preached Jesus tradition, but there was little in those reports of what Jesus said and did that would clarify the respective where and when. The evangelists, who themselves were not eyewitnesses, had a task that the preachers of Stage Two never had, namely, to shape a sequential narrative from Jesus' baptism to his resurrection. If we suppose that the first and fourth evangelists had received a form of the story of the cleansing of the temple from an intermediate source, and neither evangelist knew when it occurred during the public ministry, then each placed it where it seemed best in the sequence he was fashioning.

This leads to the insight that the Gospels have been arranged in *logical* order but not necessarily in *chronological* order. Each evangelist has ordered the material according to his understanding of Jesus and his desire to portray Jesus in a way that would meet the spiritual needs of the community he was addressing. Thus the evangelists emerge as full authors of the Gospels, shaping, developing and pruning the transmitted Jesus tradition, and as full theologians, orienting that tradition to a particular goal. The Biblical Commission *Instruction* helpfully confirms that point: "From the many things handed down, they selected some things, reduced others to a synthesis, (still) others they explicated as they kept in mind the situation of the Churches."

In the last half of the twentieth century, respect for the individuality of each Gospel had an effect on Church liturgy. Many Churches have followed the lead of the Roman Catholic liturgical reformation in introducing a three-year lectionary where the first year the Sunday Gospel readings are taken from Matthew, in the second year from Mark and in the third year from Luke. In the Catholic Church this replaced a one-year lectionary where, without any discernible theological pattern, the reading might be taken one Sunday from Matthew, another Sunday from Luke. A major factor in making the change was the recognition that Gospel selections should be read sequentially from the same Gospel if one is to do justice to the theological orientation given to those passages by the individual evangelist. For example, a parable that appears in all three Synoptic Gospels can have different meanings depending on the sequence in which each evangelist has placed it.

This means that Stage Three of Gospel formation moved the end-product Gospels still another step farther from being literal records of the ministry of Jesus (Stage One). Not only did decades of developing and adapting the Jesus tradition through preaching intervene in Stage Two, but the evangelists themselves reshaped what they received.

We are children of our time, and so we are curious about Stage One. But judgments about details of Jesus' life in the first third of the first century require painstaking scholarship; and when properly phrased, those judgments use the language of "possibly" or "probably"—rarely "certainly." Indeed, a wise caution is to be extremely skeptical when you read that some scholars are claiming that they now know exactly how much (or how little!) is literally historical in the Gospels. Most of the time they are proposing what they want to be historical to fit their own theology.

How can today's preachers, then, know what to preach, and hearers know what to believe? It is ridiculous to maintain that Christian proclamation and faith should be changed by every new vagary of scholarship. Rather, preaching and reception are to be based on Stage Three, not on uncertain theories about Stage One. In the wisdom of God we were not given eyewitness notes from Stage One but written Gospels from Stage Three, and those Gospels actually exist while scholarly reconstructions remain theoretical. *The Gospels are what was inspired by the Holy Spirit*, and Christians believe that the Holy Spirit guided the process of Gospel formation, guaranteeing that the end-product Gospels reflect the truth that God sent Jesus to proclaim.

Stage Three, if properly understood, also has consequences for more conservative Christians. In the history of biblical interpretation much time has been spent in harmonizing Gospel differences, not only in minor matters but also on a large scale. For instance, "Lives of Christ" try to make one sequential narrative out of the very different Matthean and Lucan Infancy narratives, or out of Luke's account of appearances of the risen Jesus in Jerusalem and Matthew's account of an appearance on a mountain in Galilee. Besides asking whether this harmonization is possible, we need to ask whether it is not a distortion. In the outlook of faith, Divine Providence gave us four different Gospels, not a harmonized version; and it is to the individual Gospels, each with its own viewpoint, that we should look. Harmonization, instead of enriching, impoverishes.

The "bottom line" of this discussion based on the Roman *Instruction* is that modern scholarship creates no embarrassment about the Church's traditional insistence that the Gospels are historical accounts of the ministry of Jesus, provided that, as the Church also insists, "historical" not be understood in any crassly literal sense. Indeed, the 1993 Pontifical Biblical Commission statement is harsher than the 1964 *Instruction* in criticizing undue stress on historical inerrancy and the historicizing of material that was not historical from the start.

To some Christians any thesis that does not present the Gospels as literal history implies that they are not true accounts of Jesus. Truth, however, must be evaluated in terms of the intended purpose. The Gospels might be judged untrue if the goal was strict reporting or exact biography. If the goal, however, was to bring readers/hearers to a faith in Jesus that leads them to accept God's rule or Kingdom, then adaptations that made the Gospels less than literal by adding the dimension of faith and by adjusting to new audiences facilitated that goal and thus enhanced the truth of the Gospels. The *Instruction* is lucidly clear: "The doctrine and life of Jesus were not simply reported for the sole purpose of being remembered, but were 'preached' so as to offer the Church a basis of faith and morals."

CHAPTER THREE

The Christmas Season: The Infancy Narratives

S urprisingly, in the whole New Testament only two authors pay attention to Jesus' birth and childhood: Only Matthew and Luke give us "Infancy narratives."

The first Gospel written, Mark, begins with the baptism of Jesus by John. It tells us nothing of Jesus' previous family life, never even mentioning Joseph, his legal father. In this approach Mark is far from alone in early Christianity, since the other twenty-four books of the New Testament (outside Matthew and Luke) are like Mark in failing to show interest in Jesus' family origins. Even John, who starts his Gospel not with the baptism but with the divine Word before creation ("In the beginning was the Word..."), ignores the family circumstances in which the Word became flesh and never gives us the name of Jesus' mother.

What, then, caused Matthew and Luke to begin with a story of Jesus' conception and birth? One probable factor was curiosity about the origins of this Jesus who was hailed as God's Son. Were his beginnings marked with the same divine power that later characterized his ministry? Mere curiosity, however, would not explain the two evangelists' judgment that Jesus' infancy should be made part of a written Gospel.

Neither Matthew nor Luke was composing simply a life of Jesus. Both were conveying a religious message to readers—a message that is the key to understanding the Infancy narratives. Indeed, as we shall see, despite the fact that the two evangelists fashioned very different birth stories, they agree remarkably on the religious import of the conception of

Jesus. This chapter explores the message about Jesus that Matthew and Luke sought to convey in their Infancy narratives.

How to Think About the Infancy Narratives

If it comes as a shock to many Christians to find that Matthew and Luke are our only sources of knowledge about Jesus' infancy, it may be an even greater shock to realize that the two Gospels differ so much. Our Christmas crib scenes intermix details from both Gospels; but if you pick up the New Testament without previous assumptions—without being conditioned by the customary blending of the two stories—you might be dumbfounded by the enormous difference between the first two chapters of Matthew and those of Luke.

Matthew gives a picture wherein Mary and Joseph live at Bethlehem and have a house there. The coming of the Magi guided by the star causes Herod to slay children at Bethlehem and the Holy Family to flee to Egypt. The fact that Herod's son Archelaus rules in Judea after him makes Joseph afraid to return to Bethlehem, and so he takes the child and his mother to Nazareth in Galilee—obviously for the first time.

Luke, on the other hand, tells us that Mary and Joseph lived at Nazareth and went to Bethlehem only because they had to register there during a Roman census. The statement that Mary gave birth to her child and laid him in a manger because there was no place for them in "the inn" implies that they had no house of their own in Bethlehem. And Luke's account of the peaceful return of the Holy Family from Bethlehem through Jerusalem to Nazareth leaves no room for the coming of the Magi or a struggle with Herod. Such dramatic details, so important for Matthew, have no echo in Luke.

Some scholars have tried very hard to reconcile the differences between Matthew and Luke but with little convincing success. A greater fidelity to Scripture as intended by the inspired authors would recognize that the Holy Spirit was content to give us two different accounts and that the way to interpret them faithfully is to treat them separately. Sometimes the drive to harmonize them arises from the false idea that, since Scripture is inspired, each Infancy account must be approached as if it were an exact historical account. As we saw in Chapter One, however, the Bible is a library or a collection of inspired books that contains many different types of literature, including poetry, drama, history and fiction. Indeed, between accurate history and pure fiction there is a whole range of possibilities, including imaginative retellings that have a kernel of fact.

Within that range the Infancy stories seem to differ significantly from the New Testament accounts of Jesus' ministry and death. There, known eyewitnesses, the apostles, were present to serve as the sources of the preached tradition that eventually was embodied in the Gospels. Those apostles certainly were not present at the time of the conception and birth of Jesus. Some may object that Matthew and Luke surely got their information about Jesus' birth from his parents. Yet that is never claimed in the New Testament or in the earliest Church writings, and the great difference between the two Gospel Infancy stories makes that solution improbable.

The rest of the New Testament, moreover, offers no confirming echo of what is told us in the Infancy narratives. For instance, there is no awareness of any great commotion having happened at Jesus' birth or of any revelation about Jesus' identity having been made to outsiders, such as the Magi. It is best, then, to settle for the observation that there is no way to know exactly how historical the Infancy narratives are, or to know where Matthew or Luke got them. We thus avoid both a naive fundamentalism that would take every word of these accounts as literal history, and a destructive skepticism that would reduce them to sheer mythology.

Does such a solution take away value from them? Not at all. Worrying about historicity and sources of information distracts from the inspired meaning of the biblical text, which is centered on what the two evangelists were trying to teach us, namely, the religious message on which they both agree.

We can now explore that message, which we shall divide into two major points: The first focuses on the identity of Jesus; the second, on how Jesus, in his early life, sums up the history of Israel.

The Identity of Jesus

Matthew and Luke agree that Jesus' descent is to be traced genealogically through Joseph, who was of the House of David. According to Jewish law, Joseph's acknowledgment of Jesus would make him the legal father of the child (a status not dependent on physical fatherhood), and so Jesus was truly a Son of David. Matthew and Luke agree that Mary conceived Jesus not through sexual relations with Joseph but by the creative power of the Holy Spirit. Thus Jesus was truly the Son of God. This dual identity, Son of David and Son of God, was a very important component in the New Testament understanding of *gospel* or "good news." Elsewhere in the New Testament, however, this identity is associated with moments in Jesus' life other than his conception and birth.

When Paul was writing to the Roman Christians about the year A.D. 58 and assuring this community (whom he had not converted) that he preached the same gospel that they knew, he phrased his description of Jesus as follows: "Born of the seed of David according to the flesh; designated Son of God in power according to the Holy Spirit as of resurrection from the dead" (Romans 1:3-4). Paul was pointing out the same twofold identity that we find in the Infancy narratives, but his specific emphasis was different. Writing earlier than Matthew and Luke, Paul linked Jesus' divine sonship through the Holy Spirit with the Resurrection, not with the conception of Jesus.

In Luke's account of the baptism of Jesus (3:21-22), God declares to Jesus, "You are my beloved Son," while the Holy Spirit descends on Jesus. At this very point in the Gospel, Luke presents a genealogy tracing Jesus' descent from David and the patriarchs. Once more, then, we see a twofold sonship of Jesus, from God and from David, and the activity of the Holy Spirit (now associated with the baptism).

In other words, as Christians reflected on Jesus' life, the great "moments" of that life (the resurrection, the baptism and eventually the conception) were convenient and useful occasions for clarifying who he was: the Messiah or anointed King of the House of David and the unique Son of God through the Holy Spirit. Precisely because the Infancy stories were effective vehicles of that message, they could be appropriately included in the written Gospels.

Many other essential aspects of the Gospel message about the identity of Jesus are taught us by the Infancy narratives. For instance, like the New Testament as a whole, they stress that Jesus' true identity is known only through God's revelation. In both Matthew and Luke this identity is initially proclaimed by an angel as God's messenger. Similarly, Paul insists that he did not receive his gospel from a human being, but God "was pleased to reveal his Son" (Galatians 1:12, 16). And in Matthew 16:16-17 Peter's confession of Jesus as Messiah, the Son of God, is hailed by Jesus as "not revealed by flesh and blood but by my Father in heaven." In the baptismal accounts of Mark, Matthew and Luke, God's voice speaks from heaven about the Son. In other words, there is a fundamental understanding that the identity of Jesus is a divine revelation, not a human deduction.

In the Infancy narratives, once Jesus' identity has been revealed it is quickly shared with others. In Matthew the revelation given to Joseph is in God's plan made known to the Gentile Magi. In Luke the revelation given to Mary is in God's plan made known to the Jewish shepherds. Although the cast of characters differs sharply, each evangelist in his own way is teaching us that Christ's identity is never received to be kept as a private possession. In God's providence, there are others eager to receive it, even if those others are not the ones we might have expected.

There is a negative side also to the public manifestation of Jesus' identity: a warning found in both evangelists that not all will accept the gospel, especially some who should have been eager. If the Magi come without hesitation to worship Jesus, guided by the star and (even more specifically) by the prophetic words of Scripture (see Matthew 2:2-6), the king, the chief priests and the scribes who possess the Jewish heritage and can read the Scriptures easily are quite hostile to Jesus. If Luke describes the rejoicing of the shepherds and of Simeon and Anna over the birth of "a Savior who is Christ the Lord" (2:11), there is nevertheless a solemn warning that this child is set for the fall as well as the rise of many in Israel, a sign to be contradicted who will cause the hostile thoughts of many to be revealed (2:34-35). In other words, the Christmas crib lies under the shadow of the cross; the gospel is always a factor that produces judgment; and the joy of the "good news" has also an element of sadness because not all will believe.

In a very real way, then, the Infancy narratives of Matthew and Luke are whole Gospels. They contain the basic revelation of the full identity of Jesus and the way in which this revelation was quickly shared with others, evangelizing some, but causing rejection and hatred among others.

Jesus Sums Up Israel's Story

There is a second religious message on which Matthew and Luke agree that goes beyond the identity of Jesus, and this second message may be even more necessary to proclaim today since so few Christians appreciate it. When Matthew and Luke wrote, the Scriptures in use by the Christian community were what was later called the Old Testament. (There was not yet a New Testament!) Those Scriptures were called by the Jews "the Law, the prophets and the other books."

Both Matthew and Luke used their first two chapters, the Infancy narratives, as a transition—a bridge—from these Jewish Scriptures to the story of Jesus' ministry. The evangelists made a summary of Old Testament stories and motifs and related that summary to the beginning of Jesus' life. They felt it impossible to appreciate Jesus without such preparation.

This Old Testament context is often quite foreign to

Christians today, especially to Catholic audiences. And, alas, too often they hear little preaching about it. Working with the Infancy narratives, priests and catechists might well use the Advent period to proclaim the Jewish Scriptures as a setting from which the Church begins its liturgical year. This would surely be an excellent way for us to interpret the Infancy narratives—side by side with the Church in its liturgy.

Matthew's Bridge From the Jewish Scriptures

Matthew begins his Infancy account where few Christians today would commence were they asked to tell "the story of the origin of Jesus Christ" (1:1). He begins the narrative with Abraham begetting Isaac! Matthew's record of ancestral names, in three sections (1:2-17), is far from just a list. Matthew sees the story of Jesus in the threefold story of (1) the patriarchs (Abraham to David), (2) the kings (David to the Babylonian exile) and (3) the otherwise unknown people (from the Babylonian exile to Joseph).

The strange patriarchal choices of God, who preferred as ancestors of the Messiah cheats and liars (Jacob and Judah, for example) over more honest or noble figures (such as Esau and Joseph), will be echoed by Jesus' strange choices of sinners over the just.

As for kings, there was a seeming moment of triumph when the monarchy was founded by David. But this led only to the decline of the Babylonian exile and to the loss of the kingdom and of the temple. Thus Matthew's genealogy anticipates Jesus' "upside-down" notion of the Kingdom, where his disciples are not to seek power and wherein the most dependent (like the little child) will be first.

After the Babylonian exile, Matthew gives us the unknown figures whose names follow in the list from Zerubbabel until Joseph—people too insignificant to have "made it" into the pages of biblical history. They anticipate that set of insignificant fishermen and tax collectors who will constitute the apostolic genealogy of the community that will be the heirs of Jesus.

Matthew also takes the unusual step of including women in the genealogy of Jesus. These women, moreover, are not obvious saints such as Sarah, Rebekah or Rachel but figures like Tamar (Genesis 38), Rahab (Joshua 2), Ruth and Uriah's wife Bathsheba (2 Samuel 11)—women of questionable repute or in difficult marital circumstances or seen as publicly scandalous, yet who were true instruments of God's Spirit and grace in preserving the messianic heritage and Israel. They prepare for Mary who is "found with child" before living with her husband and yet is the vessel of the Holy Spirit in conceiving Jesus.

By assembling such a complex cast of predecessors for Jesus, Matthew is preparing the reader for a similarly complex cast of those who will follow Jesus.

The rest of Matthew's Infancy narrative shows Jesus reliving even more of Israel's story than what is represented by the genealogy of the patriarchs, kings and unknown figures. When Matthew's readers heard the name Joseph, for example, they would have thought of the great Joseph, the patriarch, who was the Bible's most famous interpreter of revelation in dreams—called the "master of dreams" in Genesis 37:19—and who went down to Egypt, where he was able to save his family from famine. It is not accidental that Matthew's Joseph (of whom elsewhere the Gospels seem to know nothing other than his name) is the principal New Testament figure to receive revelation in a series of dreams and the only one to go down to Egypt.

In the Old Testament, after the patriarch Joseph brought Israel to Egypt, a wicked pharaoh killed all the Hebrew male children. The infant Moses escaped ultimately to save his people by leading them out of Egypt. Similarly, in Matthew, the wicked King Herod kills all the male children at Bethlehem. The infant Jesus (whom Matthew obviously wants to portray as another Moses) escapes ultimately to return from Egypt and save his people.

On Moses' way to the promised land, another wicked king (Balak of the Moabites) sought to employ against the Israelites a famous magus from the East, Balaam—a figure not unlike Matthew's Magi. But Balaam was moved by God to favor Israel; for in the famous episode of Balaam's ass, his visionary powers enabled him to see the star of the future Davidic king rising from Israel. Numbers 24:17 reports Balaam's prediction thus: "A star shall come forth from Jacob, and a scepter shall arise from Israel." Similarly, Matthew's Magi obey God rather than the wicked King Herod because they have seen the rising star of the true King of the Jews.

Lest Old Testament echoes in the Infancy story be missed, Matthew fortifies his narrative with frequent quotations from the prophets. For example, after the angel reveals to Joseph that Mary will bear the savior, Matthew writes that this fulfills what the Lord has said through the prophet: "The virgin shall be with child and give birth to a son, and they shall call him Emmanuel" (Isaiah 7:14). Thus in genealogy, basic narrative and formal quotation, "the Law and the prophets" (the sacred books of the Old Testament) are being applied to Jesus as the introduction to his ministry. For Matthew, Jesus sums up the whole story of Israel, to whom he has been sent.

Luke's Bridge From the Jewish Scriptures

Luke has the same attitude but works more subtly. He too begins the Infancy story with Abraham and Sarah, but not by name. Instead he portrays them in the persons of Zechariah and Elizabeth—a technique somewhat similar to a photograph which has undergone double exposure so that one set of figures is seen through another. With both Abraham/Sarah and Zechariah/Elizabeth, the situation involves the aged and barren; an angel announces the forthcoming conception to the father; the father asks, "How am I to know this?" (see Genesis 15:8); and the ultimate rejoicing of the mother is recorded.

Old Testament themes echo throughout Luke's Infancy chapters. The "canticles" or hymns of praise attributed to Mary (the Magnificat), to Zechariah (the Benedictus) and to Simeon (the Nunc Dimittis) are a mosaic of Old Testament recollections, with almost every line parallel to a verse from the prophets or psalms. In particular, the Magnificat of Mary is closely patterned on the canticle of praise that Hannah recites after the conception and birth of Samuel (1 Samuel 2:1-10).

In fact, the Hannah/Samuel story is woven throughout the Lucan Infancy narrative, for just as Hannah brought Samuel to the central sanctuary to present him to the Lord and he was received by the aged Eli (1 Samuel 1:25; 2:11), so also Mary presents Jesus at the temple sanctuary to be received by the aged Simeon. Both Jesus and Samuel are described as becoming strong and progressing in favor "before God and man" (1 Samuel 2:21, 26; Luke 2:40, 52).

Other Old Testament themes are also present in Luke's mind. There is, for instance, a strong attempt to remind us of Jesus' Davidic origins. While elsewhere the Bible identifies Jerusalem as "the city of David," Luke alone uses that title to designate Bethlehem, the birthplace of Jesus. The shepherds to whom the birth is revealed remind us that David began as a shepherd. In the story of the circumcision and presentation, Luke notes five times how the incidents of Jesus' infancy are faithful to the demands of the Jewish law. Looking at these and other details in Luke's account, we can see that his Old Testament coverage is no less comprehensive than that of Matthew, even if less systematic and obvious.

Absorbing the Twofold Message

If we read Matthew's and Luke's Infancy narratives with an eye to their twofold religious message, we shall have a magnificent access to the way these narratives function for their respective Gospels and for the Church in its liturgy. First, they tell us what we celebrate—no cloyingly sentimental "Baby Jesus" language here. Rather, we find a clear emphasis on the messianic king of the House of David and God's unique Son. Second, this identity is splendidly set in the context of Old Testament references and reminiscences to show that the God who will act through this Son as Savior and Lord behaves consistently with the way that God has acted in the past.

God has always extended gracious mercy, even to sinners. God has always lifted the lowly and has always heard the prayers of the faithful and obedient. God has always willed that the revelation given to the chosen holy ones be shared more widely for the glory of Israel and as a light to the nations.

CHAPTER FOUR

Lenten Stories From John's Gospel: Water, Light and Life

For many centuries, dating back to the ancient Jerusalem liturgy, the Church has singled out stories from John's Gospel to be read at Mass during Lent. In our era, three of these stories—the most sacred *narratives* in the Gospel accounts of Jesus' public ministry—appear on the third, fourth and fifth Sundays of Lent. They are the Samaritan woman at the well (John 4), the healing of the man born blind (John 9) and the raising of Lazarus (John 11).

These three accounts are so important liturgically that the Church grants permission for them to be read not only in the assigned year of the liturgical cycle A (1996, 1999, 2002), but in the second and third years (B, C) as well, so that there may never be a Lent in which they are not proclaimed.

Why are these stories given such prominence during Lent? Because during this season, from the earliest days, people were being prepared for Baptism, and John's stories fitted beautifully into the process of Christian initiation. In time, the three narratives were read at specific stages in the Lenten preparation of catechumens for Baptism on Holy Saturday. And as we shall see, they still serve admirably in reflecting on the implications of our own baptismal faith. To get the most from the discussion, keep your missalette or New Testament nearby so you can follow the stories in their entirety.

John's Narrative Skill

The particular genius of John's Gospel is the use of clever dramatic devices that pull readers or hearers into the action. Unlike the Gospels of Matthew, Mark and Luke, which tend to offer *brief* scenes in describing Jesus' public ministry, the Gospel of John provides lengthy encounters in which we can see how the people react to Jesus and grow in faith.

John's narratives thus lend themselves to liturgical usage. John even supplies directions for dramatization so that any of the three long stories read in Lent can easily be staged. For instance, in a double-camera technique John tells us what the Samaritan woman is saying to the villagers on a side stage while the main attention is focused on center stage where Jesus speaks to his disciples (John 4:27-39).

John wants 'you' to get engaged. The dramatic technique of John's Gospel matches its theology. Near the end of his Gospel, the evangelist states that the reason for his writing is that *"you* may believe that Jesus is the Messiah, the Son of God, and that through this belief you may have life in his name" (20:31). The evangelist is reaching out to "you" on the principle that everyone in every time and place must encounter Jesus in order to have life.

The characters described as encountering Jesus in the Gospel (the Samaritan woman, the man born blind, Martha and Mary) are in a way Everyman and Everywoman. Their encounters are narrated for your sake so that in them you may recognize yourself and be drawn into meeting Jesus in your life.

John wants us to move beyond this world. The encounter is not easy, for in John's theology Jesus has come from another world in order to reveal realities beyond human experience—realities that John calls "true" or "genuine." Yet because the Word "from above" has become flesh, the only language in which he can express his revelation is human language, the language "from below."

That can lead to confusion. For instance, Jesus speaks of water (to the Samaritan woman), sight (in reference to the blind man) and life (in the story of Lazarus); and those who encounter him think of well-known earthly concerns. In reality, however, Jesus is not speaking of earthly water that we drink only to get thirsty again, but of the water that springs up to eternal life. He is not referring to the physical sight that people can possess without being able to perceive anything they cannot touch, but to a sight into heavenly realities. He is not simply renewing a life that ends in the grave, but offering a life whereby one does not die at all.

In John's stories, then, there is a constant double level of language. Those who talk to Jesus or about him speak of what is important to them on one level (earth), while Jesus tries to lead them to another, more important level of realities (heaven). By reading these stories to us in the liturgy, the Church reminds us that Jesus is still struggling to get us to see deeper realities.

The symbols of water, sight and new life are symbols closely associated with Christian Baptism and so, as we shall discover, the stories centered on them lead us to reflect on our baptismal faith, whether we are candidates for Baptism or have already been baptized.

The Woman at the Well: Coming to Faith and Living Water

This first story (John 4:1-42) illustrates how difficult it is to come to Jesus in faith because of the various obstacles that stand in the way. If I were freely composing a story of conversion, I might imagine a central character eager to receive God. John is more realistic: Many people have a chip on their shoulder in regard to God because they feel beaten down by the inequalities in life. The woman smarts from the Jewish dislike for Samaritans, especially for Samaritan women. And that is her first obstacle to dealing with Jesus. "How can you, a Jew," she comments sarcastically, "ask me, a Samaritan woman, for a drink?"

Jesus does not answer her objection; he is not going to change instantly a whole world of injustice. Yet he can offer something that will enable the woman to put injustice in perspective, namely, living water. He means water that gives life; she misunderstands it as flowing, bubbling water, contemptuously asking him if he thinks he is greater than Jacob, who provided a well. (Is not "No thanks—I already have all I need" our first reaction when someone tries to interest us in something new religiously?)

Ironically, as John expects the reader to recognize, Jesus is greater than Jacob; but again Jesus refuses to be sidetracked from his main goal. Accordingly, he explains that he is speaking of the water that springs up to eternal life, a water that will permanently end thirst. With masterful touch John shows the woman attracted on a level of the convenience of not having to come to the well every day for water. (People are not so different today: Many are attracted to the message of those media evangelists who promote a religion that makes life more comfortable.)

To move the woman to a higher level, Jesus shifts the focus to her husband. Her reply is a half-truth, but Jesus shows that he is aware of her five husbands and of the live-in who is not her husband.

Today also, a far from perfect past is not an uncommon obstacle to conversion. To be brought to faith people must acknowledge where they stand, but they can take hope from the fact that Jesus persists even though he knows the woman's state. He does not say to the woman, "Come back after you straighten out your life," for the grace that he offers is meant to help her to change.

The Messiah is here! Confronted with Jesus' surprising knowledge of her situation, the woman seeks to take advantage of the fact that he is obviously a religious figure. Her question about whether to worship in the Jerusalem Temple or on Mount Gerizim is a typical ploy designed to distract. When is the last time she worried about such theological differences? Even today when we encounter someone who probes our lives, we are often adept at bringing up as a distraction some old religious chestnut, so as to avoid making a decision.

Once more Jesus refuses to be sidetracked. Although

salvation is from the Jews, a time is coming and is now here when such an issue is irrelevant: Cult at both sites will be replaced by worship in Spirit and truth. Nimbly the woman tries one more ploy by shifting any decision to the distant future when the Messiah comes, but Jesus will not let her escape. His "I am he" confronts her with a current demand for faith.

The disciples, too, must dig deeper. What follows, enacted dramatically on two stages, reveals even more about faith. In center stage we observe that the disciples, who have now been with Jesus some time, understand his heavenly symbolism no better than the woman who encountered him for the first time. When he speaks of the food that he already has to eat, they wonder if someone has brought him a sandwich! Jesus has to explain: "My food is to do the will of the One who sent me..." (John 4:34).

On side stage, we find that the woman is still not fully convinced since she poses to the villagers the question, "Could this be the Messiah?" The villagers come and encounter Jesus for themselves so that their faith is not simply dependent on her account but on personal contact. We are left to surmise that by being instrumental in bringing others to believe, the woman's own faith came to completion. And at last she drank of the water of life.

The Man Born Blind: Faith Grows Amid Trials

If the story of the Samaritan woman has illustrated an initial coming to faith, this next carefully crafted narrative (John 9:1-41) shows that often first enlightenment does not result in adequate faith. *Sometimes faith comes only through difficult testing and even suffering.*

Saint Augustine recognized that this man born blind stands for the human race. And the initial dialogue where Jesus proclaims, "I am the light of the world," alerts us to the fact that more than physical sight is involved.

The basic story of the man's healing is simple. Jesus approaches the blind man, anoints his eyes with mud mixed with saliva and tells him to wash in the Pool of Siloam. The man does so and comes back seeing.

Beyond this, however, the early Christian community who first heard John's account probably picked out elements of their own conversion and Baptism in the blind man's story. They might recognize something familiar, for example, in the blind man's coming to see the light by being "anointed." Anointing became a part of Baptism very early, and "enlightenment" was a term for baptismal conversion, as we see in Hebrews 6:4; 10:32 and in the second-century writer Justin.

John hints further that the water has a special link with Christ since he tells us that "Siloam," the name of the pool, means "the One sent," a frequent description of Jesus. No wonder that in early catacomb art the healing of the blind man was a symbol of Baptism.

Besides recognizing a baptismal theme in this story, readers of John would also be taught that a series of testings may be necessary before sight really comes. Only gradually and through suffering does the man born blind come to full faith and enlightenment.

There are at least four steps in his progress, each involving an encounter: (1) At first, when queried by the onlookers, the man born blind knows only that "the man they call Jesus" healed him (9:11). (2) Then, brought before the Pharisees and pressed with theological questions, he advances to the conclusion that Jesus is "a prophet" (9:17). (3) Next, after being threatened with expulsion from the synagogue, he recognizes that Jesus is a man "from God" (9:33). (4) Finally, having been expelled, he encounters Jesus himself, who has sought him out and now asks point blank, "Do you believe in the Son of Man?" It is then at last that the man says, "I do believe" (9:38: perhaps the baptismal confession required in the Johannine Church).

How many of us who have a traditional faith stemming from our Baptism come to believe in our hearts only when difficult decisions test our faith in God and Christ? It is then we understand what it means to say, "I do believe."

A rift among the Pharisees over Jesus' interpretation of the sabbath. Yet it is not only from the man born blind that we learn about faith. His being healed produces a division (Greek *krisis*, whence the English "crisis") among those who interrogate him. In the Johannine view an encounter with Jesus or his work forces people to decide and align themselves on one side or the other.

Particularly interesting is the division caused among the Pharisees (9:13-17). John presents favorably those Pharisees who decide that Jesus cannot be sinful because he does such signs (healings), but we should also seek to understand the other Pharisees who decide that Jesus is not from God because he does not keep the sabbath.

Their thinking probably went along these lines: God commanded that the sabbath be kept holy; our ancestors decided that kneading clay was menial work that violated the sabbath; Jesus kneaded clay on the sabbath and so he violated God's commandment. Might not faithful Christians today judge along similar lines if someone violated what they had been taught as a traditional interpretation of God's will? (And might they not be offended if their decisions were greeted with the sarcasm with which the man born blind reacted to the Jewish authorities' decision about Jesus?)

The difficulty with such reasoning is the failure to recognize that all human interpretations of God's will are historically conditioned—those we regard as definitive tradition are *true*, but *in regard to the issues that were in mind when they were formulated*. The Hebrews as slaves in Egypt had to work with clay to make bricks for the Pharaoh, and so kneading clay would justly be classified as servile work forbidden on the sabbath. But those who made that classification scarcely thought of kneading a scrap of clay to open a blind man's eyes.

Jesus is the type of figure who raises new religious issues and inevitably causes offense to those who attempt to solve those issues quickly on the basis of previous situations. Recognition of that should facilitate important insights. It was not necessarily out of malice that many of the genuinely religious people of Jesus' time (who were Jews because of where he lived) rejected him. If Jesus came back today, he would be equally offensive to religious people of our time, including Christians. We should be careful about religious judgments that apply, without nuance, past decisions to *new* situations.

The blind man's parents: trying to dodge the issue. Finally, we can learn about faith from the parents of the blind man. John contrasts the man born blind who, step by step, was brought to sight physically and spiritually, with the opposing religious authorities, who could see physically but gradually became blind spiritually (9:40-41). Yet the evangelist is also interested in those who refuse to commit themselves one way or the other. The parents know the truth about their son, but they refuse to say anything about what Jesus has done for him lest they be thrown out of the synagogue.

Today there are those who decide for Jesus at a great cost to themselves, and those who for various reasons do not believe in him. Perhaps an even larger group would be those who have been baptized and nominally accept Jesus but are not willing to confess him if it costs anything. In John's view that is as serious as to deny him.

The Raising of Lazarus: Faith Tested by Death

As we come to the final narrative (John 11:1-44), we should take note of the different staging techniques in the three stories. The Samaritan woman remained close to Jesus for much of the drama at the well and entered into a fairly long dialogue with him. The man born blind said nothing to Jesus at the beginning, was not in contact with him through most of the scene, and exchanged words with Jesus only at the end in a moment of piercing light when he confessed Jesus. Lazarus never says a word to Jesus (or anyone else) and appears only in the last verses.

In each story we are dealing with a different stage of faith. The Samaritan woman illustrated an initial coming to faith; the man born blind illustrated an incipient faith that acquired depth only after testing; the Lazarus story illustrates *the deepening of faith that comes through an experience of death.*

John tells the Lazarus story in such a way that, along with the disciples and Martha and Mary, we are led to a deeper understanding of Lazarus' death. Like his sisters Martha and Mary, Lazarus was loved by Jesus; and so when he dies, the disciples are troubled by Jesus' seeming indifference. They misunderstand when he speaks of Lazarus' sleep. As with blindness in John 9 (of which we are reminded in 11:37), life and death are used to teach about earthly and heavenly realities.

Martha, the chief dialogue partner in the drama, already believes that Jesus is the Messiah, the Son of God, and that her brother Lazarus will participate in the resurrection on the last day. Yet hers is an incomplete faith, for she wishes that her brother had never died and hesitates when Jesus orders Lazarus' tomb opened.

Jesus can and does bring Lazarus back to earthly life, but that is not his purpose in having come to this world from above. (A man brought back from the grave is not necessarily better off or closer to God than those who have not yet died.) Jesus comes *to give life that cannot be touched by death,* so that those who believe in him will never die (11:26). True faith has to include a belief in Jesus as the source of unending life. Such immortality, however, cannot come in Jesus' public ministry; it awaits Jesus' own resurrection.

Signs of the deeper life still to come. Consequently, we encounter more unexplained symbolism in the Lazarus narrative than was present in the stories of the Samaritan woman and the man born blind. We are never told, for instance, that Martha and Mary came to understand fully Jesus' words, "I am the life."

In another instance, we hear that Jesus shuddered, seemingly with anger, when he saw Mary and her Jewish friends weeping. But the evangelist does not clarify why Jesus reacts in this way at what seems like well-intentioned grief (11:33, 38).

Nor does John supply an interpretation of why Lazarus

emerges from the tomb tied hand and foot with burial bands and his face wrapped in a cloth (11:44). Only when we read the account of Jesus' tomb in 20:6-7 does that symbolism become clear. Jesus rises to eternal life, never to die again; therefore he leaves behind in the tomb his burial wrappings and the piece that covered his head, for which he has no need. Lazarus was brought back to life enveloped in burial clothes because he was going to die again.

Thus, although the raising of Lazarus is a tremendous miracle bringing to culmination Jesus' ministry, it is still a sign. The life to which Lazarus is raised is natural life; it is meant to symbolize eternal life, the kind of life that only God possesses and that Jesus as God's Son makes possible.

Facing our own final test. How does this fit into Lenten reflections on faith? Even after the struggles of initial faith (the Samaritan woman) and a faith made mature through testing (the man born blind), facing death often constitutes a unique challenge to belief. Whether the death of a loved one or one's own death, it is the moment where one realizes that all depends on God. No human support goes with one to the grave; credit cards, health insurance, retirement programs and human companionship stop at the tomb. One enters alone.

If there is no God, there is nothing; if Christ has not conquered death, there is no future. The brutality of that realization causes trembling even among those who have spent their lives professing Christ. It is not unusual for people to confess that doubts have come into their minds as they face death.

Paul cries out that death is the last enemy to be overcome (1 Corinthians 15:26), an insight that John captures by placing the Lazarus story at the end of Jesus' public ministry. From it we learn that no matter how fervently catechumens or already baptized Christians make or renew a baptismal profession in Lent, they may still face a last moment when their faith will be tested.

It will be precisely at that moment, when we are confronted with the visible reality of the grave, that we need to hear and embrace the bold message that Jesus proclaims in

John's Gospel: "I am the life." Despite all human appearances, "Everyone who believes in me shall never die at all."

We began Lent with the reminder that we will return to dust. We end at Easter with the proclamation of new life.

CHAPTER FIVE

Holy Week:
The Passion Narratives

E very Holy Week the liturgy of the Church issues a real
challenge even to some of the most serious readers of the
Bible. It does this by appointing two different Passion
narratives to be read within a short period. A week before
Easter, on Palm or Passion Sunday, we hear the Passion
according to Matthew (Year A) or Mark (Year B) or Luke (Year
C); on Good Friday every year the Passion according to John
is read. If you examine these Passion accounts carefully, you
will notice that the two narratives which are read do not give
the same picture of Jesus' death in terms either of content or
of outlook. John, for example, presents a Jesus of kingly
serenity, while Mark's stark portrait of Jesus emphasizes the
depths of abandonment before his final triumph.

This can be quite a shocking discovery for some people!
They may well wonder: How can the inspired writers give us
different versions of the same event? Is there distortion or
error? Has God's word contradicted itself? We can get back to
these concerns later in this chapter. But before we do that, we
need to see how the Passion accounts were written and to
explore the dramatic, pastoral and theological factors that
colored their composition. (In the next chapter we shall
discuss some historical elements that played a role.)

Gospel Writers Began With Jesus' Death and Resurrection

In Chapter Two we saw three stages of Gospel formation
and how the written Gospels were shaped by the oral

preaching that preceded them. In that preaching, it has been argued, the emphasis on aspects of Jesus' life moved chronologically backward, starting from his resurrection and working toward his birth. Early Christian preaching certainly paid primary attention to the crucifixion and resurrection. For example, the Acts of the Apostles repeats this theme: "You killed Jesus by hanging or crucifying him, but God raised him up" (2:32, 36; 5:30-31; 10:39-40). Then, as Christians reflected on the earlier career of the crucified one, accounts of Jesus' public ministry emerged, and eventually (in Matthew and Luke) accounts of his birth. Thus, a basic account of the crucifixion may have been shaped relatively soon in Gospel formation.

The shaping of such an account would have been facilitated by the necessary order of the events. Arrest had to precede trial, which, in turn, had to precede sentence and execution. The result in our Gospels is a true narrative with a development of plot, tracing the actions and reactions not only of Jesus, but also of a cast of surrounding characters, such as Peter, Judas and Pilate. The impact of Jesus' fate on various people is vividly illustrated, and even when we read the Passion accounts today we notice how the drama of the tragedy has been heightened by contrasting one character with another. For example, alongside the innocent Jesus who is condemned is the revolutionary Barabbas who is freed, even though guilty of a political charge similar to that levied against Jesus. Alongside the scoffing Jewish authorities who make fun of the crucified Jesus as Messiah or Son of God is a Roman soldier who recognizes him as Son of God. No wonder that the liturgy encourages us to act out the Passion narratives by reading assigned roles aloud! Each Passion narrative constitutes a simple dramatic play.

Indeed, it is almost as if John gives stage directions when he describes the trial of Jesus before Pilate. He has the chief priests and "the Jews" carefully localized outside the praetorium (the Roman procurator's court) while Jesus is alone within. Then he shows Pilate shuttling back and forth between the two sides, clearly dramatizing a man who seeks to take a middle position, reconciling what he regards as extremes rather than deciding for either. Yet the tables are turned; Pilate is presented in such a way that he, not Jesus, is the one really on trial, caught between light and darkness, truth and falsehood. Jesus challenges him to hear the truth (John 18:37); and his cynical response, "What is truth?" is really a decision for falsehood. John is warning the reader that no one can avoid judgment when he or she stands before Jesus.

Audience Participation Invited

Because of the dramatic format of the Passion accounts, it is easy for us to step into the shoes of the different character types we meet there. Thus drama facilitates the pastoral concern of the evangelists to reach out to their hearers or readers. We feel drawn, in fact, to participate by asking ourselves how we would have stood in relation to the trial and crucifixion of Jesus. With which character in the narrative would I identify myself? The distribution of palms in church may too quickly assure me that I would have been among the crowd that hailed Jesus appreciatively. Is it not more likely that I might have been among the disciples who fled from danger, abandoning him? At moments in my life have I not played the role of Peter, denying Jesus, or even of Judas, betraying him? Have I not found myself like the Pilate of John's Gospel, trying to avoid a decision between good and evil? Or like the Pilate of Matthew's account, have I made a bad decision and then washed my hands so that the record could show that I was blameless?

Or, most likely of all, might I not have stood among the religious people who disliked Jesus? If this possibility seems remote, it is because many have oversimplified the motives of Jesus' opponents. In the next chapter I shall point out how and why the Gospel accounts have given a simplified portrayal of those who decided on Jesus' death, especially the Jewish leaders. Historically it would be astounding if there were not among them some venal "ecclesiastical" politicians who were getting rid of a possible danger to their own position. (The Annas high-priestly family of which Caiaphas was a member gets low marks in Jewish memory.) It would be equally amazing if the majority did not consist of sincerely religious men who thought they were serving God in ridding Israel of a troublemaker like Jesus (see John 16:2). In their view Jesus may have been a false prophet misleading people by his permissive attitudes toward the sabbath and sinners. The Jewish mockery of Jesus after the Sanhedrin trial makes his status as a prophet the issue (Mark 14:65) and, according to the law of Deuteronomy 13:1-6, the false prophet had to be put to death lest he seduce Israel from the true God.

In assigning ourselves a role in the Passion story, how might we have been among the opponents of Jesus? Gospel readers are often sincerely religious people who have a deep attachment to what they were taught. Jesus was a challenge to religious traditionalists because he asked people to change their minds and at times he questioned human elements in the tradition that had been given divine status as God's will (see Matthew 15:6). If Jesus were to appear today, it is quite likely that he would continue to upset literal-minded religious people of our time. Not Jewish background but religious mentality is the basic component in the reaction to Jesus.

Theological Factors in the Death of Jesus

Besides reflecting on the dramatic and pastoral elements in the Passion of Jesus, we should be attuned to the theological factors that shaped the Gospel narratives. They were written to depict the role of Jesus in God's plan. We may begin by asking how the passion fitted into Jesus' ministry of proclaiming God. We are told in Romans 4:25 that Jesus died for our sins, but would Jesus himself have used such language? Did he foresee the exact manner of his death and victory?

In Mark (8:31, 9:31-32, 10:33-34) there are three predictions of the fate of the Son of Man, one more detailed than the other. Yet, once we are aware of the Church's official teaching (explained in Chapter Two) that sayings uttered by Jesus were expanded and interpreted by the apostolic preachers and the evangelists before they were put in the Gospels, we have the right and duty to ask whether these predictions have not become more exact by hindsight. Have they not been filled out with details by those who knew what happened to Jesus? John has three statements (3:14; 8:28; 12:32-34) about the "lifting up" of the Son of Man—a much less precise reference to crucifixion and ascension! Thus Jesus may have originally expressed general premonitions about his suffering and death (a hostile fate discoverable from the example of the prophets), plus a firm trust that God would make him victorious (without knowing exactly how).

Hebrews 5:7-8 reports, "In the days when he was in the flesh, he offered prayers and supplications with clamor and tears to the One who was able to save him from death, and he was heard because of his fear. Son though he was, he learned obedience from what he suffered." Jesus had preached that God's Kingdom would be realized most readily when human beings acknowledged their dependence on God. The model for this Kingdom was not power over others but the helplessness of the little child. We humans come most clearly to terms with our helplessness when we face death. Did Jesus, the proclaimer of the Kingdom, himself have to experience the vulnerability of dying before the Kingdom could be achieved in and through him? Jesus' reference at the Last Supper (Luke 22:16, 18) to the imminence of the Kingdom confirms the possibility that he used "Kingdom" language to phrase his own understanding of his death.

The coming of the Kingdom would involve the ultimate destruction of the power of evil, and Jesus' confrontation with Satan in the great period of trial is echoed in various Passion narrative passages (Mark 14:38; Luke 22:53; John 14:30). The thought of such a confrontation may explain Jesus' anguish before his fate, and his trust in God's power to defeat Satan may have been his way of expressing the truth caught by New Testament writers when, in the language of Christian theology, they said that he died to remove sin.

Besides reflecting on what Jesus' Passion meant to him in his understanding of his ministry (so far as we can reconstruct that from the Gospels) we should also ask how it was understood theologically by Christians of the New Testament period. We can be guided here by what the four Gospels underline in portraying the Passion. It is noteworthy that many features depicted by later artists and writers have no place in the Gospel accounts, for instance, elements of pathos and emotion, and a concentration on pain and suffering. On Calvary the evangelists report laconically, "They crucified him," without reference to the manner.

Strikingly, however, they pay attention to dividing his garments and to the exact placement of the criminals crucified with him. Such details were important to the early Christians because they found them anticipated in Old Testament psalms and prophets. Not biography but a theology of God's plan dominated the choice of events to be narrated. In other words, by linking what happened to Jesus with passages of the Jewish Scriptures, the Gospel writers were trying to explain the rich meaning of Jesus' actions. We must remember that the Old Testament was the theological source book of the time. The evangelists were emphasizing that through the Scriptures of Israel God had taught about his Son. In the last third of the first century, when the evangelists wrote, their emphasis can also be seen as an argument against those Jews who rejected the crucified Jesus precisely because they did not think he fulfilled scriptural expectations.

Different Gospel Views of Jesus' Death

Moving beyond the shared theology, we find a distinctive insight in each Passion account. Attention to the individual Passion narratives may be very helpful when we read and hear the two that the Church chooses for Holy Week in a given year.

Mark's version: Despite human rejection Jesus is vindicated. Mark's Passion narrative portrays a stark human abandonment of Jesus that is reversed dramatically at the end. From the moment Jesus moves to the Mount of Olives, the behavior of the disciples is negatively portrayed. While Jesus prays, they fall asleep three times. Judas betrays him and Peter curses, denying knowledge of him. All flee, with the last one leaving even his clothes behind in order to get away from Jesus—the opposite of leaving all things to follow him. Both Jewish and Roman judges are presented as cynical. Jesus hangs on the cross for six hours, three of which are filled with human mockery, while in the second three the land is covered with darkness. Jesus' only word from the cross is: "My God, my God, why have you forsaken me?" and even that plaintive cry is met with derision. Yet, as Jesus breathes his last, God acts to confirm the Son. The trial before the Jewish Sanhedrin had concerned Jesus' threat to destroy the temple sanctuary and his claim to be the messianic Son of the Blessed One. At Jesus' death the veil of the sanctuary is rent, and a Roman centurion confesses, "Truly this was God's Son." After the cross it is possible, then, to see that Jesus was not a false prophet.

Matthew's version: A vivid portrayal of the participants. The longest of the four, this follows closely the main lines of Mark's narrative, although the theme of abandonment is less prominent amid the flow of the additional material, which dramatizes the participants in an unforgettable way. The character of Judas is greatly developed. After Peter's predicted denials, Matthew alone makes clear that another prediction is fulfilled: It would have been better for Judas not to have been born. Like Ahithophel, David's trusted adviser who went over to David's enemies and then hung himself (2 Samuel 15—17), Judas hangs himself, professing regret that he has given over innocent blood. The dramatic theme of who is responsible for that blood runs through the material that is found only in Matthew's Passion narrative. The chief priests will not accept Judas' blood money into the treasury. On the basis of a dream Pilate's wife tells her husband to have nothing to do with that just man; and Pilate washes his hands, declaring that he is innocent of Jesus' blood. Drawing on phrasing from Jeremiah 26:8, 15 (for example, "It is innocent blood that you bring on yourselves, this city, and its citizens"), Matthew has "all the people" take responsibility on themselves and their children. The fact that the next generation is included probably means that Matthew thinks that what was done to Jesus brought about the destruction of Jerusalem forty years later.

The death of Jesus is marked by remarkable signs indicating that God's judgment on the world has begun. Not only is the sanctuary veil rent (as in Mark); but also the earth is shaken, the rocks are rent, the tombs opened and the saints who were asleep raised. These vivid scenes, peculiar to Matthew, continue at the Resurrection, as an earthquake paralyzes the guards who have been set at the tomb to block the Resurrection. Thus God's power frustrates the plans of Pilate, the chief priests and the scribes. The final line of that story, which claims that a lie has been spread among Jews until this day, betrays the bad feelings between Matthew's Church and Jewish authorities that govern much of this material not found in Mark—feelings that, as we shall see in the next chapter, we must be very careful to correct today.

Luke's version: Jesus embodies forgiveness for others. Luke's portrayal is quite different. The disciples appear in a more sympathetic light, for they have remained faithful to Jesus in his trials (22:28). In Gethsemane if they fall asleep (once, not thrice), it is because of sorrow. Even enemies fare better: No false witnesses are produced by the Jewish authorities, and three times Pilate acknowledges that Jesus is not guilty. The people are on Jesus' side, grieving over what has been done to him. Jesus himself is less anguished by his fate than by his concern for others. He heals the slave's ear at the time of the arrest; on the road to Calvary he worries about the fate of the women; he forgives those who crucified him; and he promises Paradise to the penitent "thief" (a figure peculiar to Luke). The crucifixion becomes the occasion of divine forgiveness and care; and Jesus dies tranquilly, praying, "Father, into your hands I commit my spirit."

That kind of death anticipates the death of Stephen in Acts

7:59, since the first one to die for Christ asks forgiveness for those who stone him and prays, "Lord Jesus, receive my spirit." Similarly, Pilate's sending Jesus to Herod during the Lucan account of the trial anticipates Acts 25:13—26:32 where, during the trial of Paul, the Roman governor Festus presents him to the Herodian King Agrippa II. In both cases the Jewish king confirms the Roman judgment of innocence. Among the evangelists only Luke has written a second book, the Acts of the Apostles, to complement the Gospel; and he wants readers to see parallelism between what happened to Jesus and what happened to the great Christian heroes like Stephen and Paul who took up their cross and followed him.

John's version: Jesus reigns even from the cross. John's Passion narrative presents a sovereign Jesus who has defiantly announced, "I lay down my life to take it up again; no one has taken it from me" (10:17-18). When Roman soldiers and Jewish police come to arrest him, they fall to the earth powerless as he speaks the divine phrase, "I am." In the garden he does not pray to be delivered from the hour of trial and death as he does in the other Gospels, for the hour is the whole purpose of his life (12:27). His self-assurance is an offense to the high priest (18:22); and Pilate is afraid before the Son of God who states, "You have no power over me" (19:8, 11).

No Simon of Cyrene appears, for the Jesus of John carries his own cross. His royalty is proclaimed in three languages and confirmed by Pilate. Unlike the portrayal in the other Gospels, Jesus is not alone on Calvary, for at the foot of the cross stand the Beloved Disciple and the Mother of Jesus. He relates these two highly symbolic figures to each other as son and mother, thus leaving behind a family of believing disciples. Jesus does not cry out, "My God, why have you forsaken me?" because the Father is always with him (16:32). Rather, his final words are a solemn decision, "It is finished." Only when he has decided does he hand over his spirit. Even in death he dispenses life as water flows from within him (see 7:38-39). His burial is not unprepared as in the other Gospels; rather, thanks to Nicodemus, he lies amid a hundred pounds of spices as befits a king.

When these different Passion narratives are read side by side, one should not be upset by the contrasting accounts or ask which view of Jesus is more correct: the Jesus in Mark, who plumbs the depths of abandonment only to be vindicated; the Jesus of Matthew, who is an innocent victim, the responsibility for whose death touches many; the Jesus of Luke, who worries about others and gently dispenses forgiveness; or the Jesus in John's account, who reigns victoriously from the cross, in control of all that happens. All four are given to us by the inspiring Spirit, and no one of them exhausts the meaning of Jesus. It is as if one walks around a large diamond to look at it from four different angles. A true picture of the whole emerges only because the viewpoints are different.

The Passion Narratives and Anti-Judaism

A s explained in the previous chapter, part of what makes
Holy Week holy is the solemn reading of two Gospel
Passion narratives. These masterpieces have given more
inspiration to artists, musicians, poets and mystics than any
other sections of the New Testament. Ironically, however, such
dramatic power makes sensitive Christians uneasy about anti-
Jewish elements in the Passion narratives. How can they be
proclaimed without adding to the tragic history of their
misuse against the Jewish people?

In my two-volume commentary on the Passion narratives,
The Death of the Messiah (Doubleday, 1994), my primary focus
was the positive message that the evangelists wished to
convey to their Christian hearers and readers. I gave
considerable attention to the danger of anti-Judaism in our
reactions. In this chapter I want to concentrate on the
evolution of anti-Judaism in New Testament thought about
the Passion. Looking at how anti-Jewish sentiment developed
gradually after Jesus' day can help us to understand how our
earliest religious ancestors approached the death of Jesus. In
part this will require observations about the historicity of the
Passion narratives, an area that was deliberately left aside in
the previous chapter.

Two Faulty Interpretations of the Passion Narratives

Careful study of the Scriptures should lead us to object
strongly to two faulty interpretations of the Passion

narratives: viewing them either (1) as literal history or (2) as a product of Christian imagination.

Objections to the literal history view. Throughout the centuries and still today, a literal interpretation has produced a view of the Jewish leaders as scheming liars who knowingly deceived the Roman prefect in order to bring about Jesus' death. Matthew's and John's use of the generalizing description of these opponents of Jesus as "Jews," admittedly a hostile description reflecting situations in the first century, has too often been heard as referring to Jews of later centuries. That was not at all the intention of Matthew or John.

This misreading, which has contributed to ongoing hate, has now been firmly rejected in Roman Catholicism, whether or not all Catholics know it. As we saw in Chapter Two, in 1964 the Roman Pontifical Biblical Commission taught authoritatively that the Gospels are the product of considerable development—narrative, organizational and theological development. They are not simply literal accounts of the ministry of Jesus. The next year Vatican Council II explicitly condemned an outlook that would blame the Passion without distinction on all the Jews then living or on the Jews today. (See the Council's 1965 *Declaration on the Relationship of the Church to Non-Christian Religions*, #4.)

Objections to the 'Christian invention' interpretation. The other view I judge unacceptable discredits the Gospel Passion narratives as almost totally the product of Christian imagination. Under the mantle of scholarly objectivity, advocates assert firmly but without proof that the early Christians knew little about how Jesus died and simply invented their narratives on the basis of Old Testament imagery.

Indeed, some scholars (of Christian upbringing!) would paint the early Christians as creating lies precisely to vilify the Jews. Yet if the literalist interpretation of the Passion narratives can produce hate toward Judaism, this "imagination interpretation" can have the effect of portraying Christianity as a false and hateful religion. Religiously sensitive Jews and Christians recognize that if either group of our respective first-century ancestors—Jews or Christians—is presented as liars who wanted to destroy their opposites, nothing has been gained in the ongoing Jewish-Christian dialogue.

A careful examination suggests that the situation in the first century was far more complex than such overly simple reconstructions allow. Let me attempt to do at least partial justice to the complexities by describing *four stages* in the development of New Testament attitudes toward the death of Jesus, beginning with the first stage: the likely historical facts.

Stage One: What Really Happened to Jesus?

Without repeating all the evidence amassed in *The Death of the Messiah*, a very plausible case can be made for the following: Jesus upset and even alarmed certain of his co-religionists by his attitudes toward some legal demands, his assumptions about his own unique teaching authority, his association with sinners and his critique of public practices that he regarded as meaningless religiosity.

Rumors that he might be the Messiah (whether promoted by friends or opponents) caused tension. This came to a head when in Jerusalem he criticized temple procedures and threatened the sanctuary—a sensitive issue economically, socially and politically. A Sanhedrin, or meeting, involving the high priest and other important Jerusalem figures, called to deal with Jesus, is described differently in the different Gospels. In Mark (and in Matthew and partly in Luke, drawing on Mark) it takes place on the night Jesus was arrested and thus just before he died; in John 11:47-53 it takes place long before and Jesus is not even present. Mark's picture may well be a simplification to create a balance between a Jewish and a Roman trial, but what is more important in judging historicity is the issue on which the different accounts agree. A Sanhedrin decided that Jesus was a dangerous and arrogant (that is to say, blasphemous) nuisance and ultimately arranged for him to be seized and handed over to the Roman authorities.

That Jesus could have been manhandled and abused in such an arrest and transferal, as all the Gospels maintain, would be far from surprising. For the Roman governor he was not a major threat. (Pilate's prefecture up to this time saw occasional protests and riots but not the armed revolutionary movements of earlier or later periods, when the Romans sent out troops and executed hundreds without any pretense at trial.) Nevertheless, Jesus was potentially a menace if people thought he was a messiah or king, and so Pilate ordered Jesus executed.

The historical plausibility of this Gospel picture can be supported from Josephus, the Jewish historian who wrote his *Antiquities* at the end of the first century A.D. Amid his account of Pilate's governorship (including several instances of crowds assembling to put pressure on him), Josephus refers to Pilate's treatment of Jesus. Serious scholarship would now accept the following as authentically written by Josephus: Jesus was a wise man who did astonishing deeds and taught many people, but "Pilate condemned him to the cross on indictment of the first-ranking men among us."

From Josephus' description of what happened thirty years later to another man called Jesus (the son of Ananias), we learn how such an indictment might have worked. This other Jesus cried out a message against Jerusalem and the temple sanctuary. By such behavior he provoked the leading citizens who, thinking he was under some supernatural drive, had him beaten and led him before the Roman governor. The latter had him scourged, but he would not respond. (He was finally let go as a maniac but was killed in the siege of Jerusalem.) A combination of the Josephus accounts shows how exaggerated are the assertions that the substance of the Gospel portrayals of the treatment of Jesus of Nazareth, as described above, cannot be historical.

Stage Two: Christian Interpretation

Neither the claim of wholesale invention nor the literalist

failure to recognize creative rethinking does justice to what happened next. The New Testament is insistent that what befell Jesus matched what was found in the Law and the prophets. Memories preserved by Jesus' followers were colored in particular by the Old Testament portraits of how the just suffered at the hands of the wicked.

Historically, the motives of the authorities aligned against Jesus at the time of his execution were surely a mixture: genuine religious outrage at his actions and claims, worry about civic unrest, crass self-interest, fear of his provoking Roman intervention, and so on.

Yet by the time the Gospels were being written we see a quest for simplification, motivated by theological reasons: Those opposed to Jesus took on the biblical coloring of the wicked who plot against the innocent. In Wisdom 2:17-21, for instance, the wicked contend that if the just one be the son of God, God will defend him; and they resolve to revile him and put him to death. The abuse and travail of Jesus take on the plaintive tones of the hymnist of Psalm 22 and the Suffering Servant of Isaiah 52—53. For his followers, Jesus' sufferings cast light on such passages, which illumined the role of Jesus' death in the plan of God.

This stage of reflection on the Passion was not anti-Jewish, any more than were the psalms or other biblical books that were mined for the imagery. The just one, his admirers and the wicked opponents were all Jews, after all. And the theological simplification of the opponents as wicked is a standard biblical portrayal, not a nefarious Christian falsification.

Six hundred years before, not all who disagreed with Jeremiah's policies for Judah were wicked; but the biblical account portrays them thus, simplifying their motives and dramatizing their actions. Indeed some of the most sensitive words in the Passion of Jesus are found in Jeremiah 26. When, with God's authority, Jeremiah threatened the destruction of the temple, the priests and *all the people* heard him, and the priests and the prophets demanded his death. Jeremiah warned them that they were bringing *innocent blood* on

Jerusalem and its citizens.

Stage Three: Distinguishing 'the Jews' From 'the Romans'

We can tell from Paul's writings that the conversion of Gentiles to Jesus became a major factor in early Christianity. The apostle encountered hostility from synagogue authorities in his proclamation of the Gospel, as he indicates in 2 Corinthians 11:24 ("From the Jews on five occasions I received the thirty-nine lashes"), and so did his Gentile converts, according to Acts.

Paul compared the enmity Christians were experiencing to that endured by Jesus, employing in 1 Thessalonians 2:14-15 a description of "*the Jews who killed the Lord Jesus* and the prophets and who persecuted us." In itself, that could be simply a distinguishing classification (those Jews who had a role in Jesus' death, as distinct from other Jews). But two decades after Jesus' death his Passion was entering into debates between Jews who did not accept Jesus and Jews and Gentiles who did.

How much anti-Judaism was involved in this use of the word *Jews* for the Jerusalem authorities who had a role in Jesus' death? A number of factors governed the issue. For instance, how much hostility did readers or hearers experience from Jews who rejected the proclamation of Jesus? At this early period Christian Jews who used such language may at other times have been nostalgic about their Jewish heritage (as Paul was in Romans 9:3-5).

The same would not have been true of Gentile Christians. Indeed they may have read into an expression like "the Jews who killed the Lord Jesus" prejudices against Jews stemming from their own Gentile background.

Was equal hostility showed by Christians toward the Romans who had a role in the death of Jesus? It probably depended on whether Roman authority had harried the Christians. The psalm application in Acts 4:25-27 places in equal array against Jesus "Herod and Pontius Pilate, the Gentiles and the peoples of Israel." In the Gospel portrayals, the mockery of Jesus by Roman soldiers is more brutal than that by Jewish authorities or police.

Stage Four: 'The Jews' Did It

Paul's phrase "the Jews who killed Jesus" was restrictive to one group of Jews. Before long such language became generalized, particularly as at different places in different moments Gentile Christians outnumbered Christians of Jewish ethnicity. More delicately, because of alienation (and at times expulsion) from synagogues, some ethnically Jewish Christians were no longer using the term "Jews" of themselves. That seems to be the case among some of the Christians reflected in the Gospels of John and Matthew.

Accordingly, when a major role in Jesus' Passion was attributed to "the Jews," the impression was now being given that another people (different from us Christians) was involved. The passage in Matthew, "All the people said, 'His blood on us and on our children'" (27:25) was read to mean that these other people were taking on the responsibility for the death of Jesus. Indeed, the reference to "children" here and in Luke 23:28 ("Daughters of Jerusalem...for yourselves weep and for your children") suggests that the Roman defeat of the Jews and the destruction of the Jerusalem temple in A.D. 70 were perceived as God's punishment for having put Jesus to death.

It is not surprising that Christians would make such a judgment, given that the Jewish historian Josephus gave an analogous theological explanation: God turned away from Jerusalem and allowed the Romans to burn the city because of hate for the impiety, murders and profanation among Jews there in the 50's and 60's.

Alleviating factors such as some Christians' nostalgia for their Jewish past was now gone: The parallel became complete between "the Jews" who were hostile to Jesus and contemporary Jews who did not accept Jesus and were considered hostile. Echoes of that attitude are heard in the passage in John 19:12 where "the Jews" cry out, "If you release this man, you are not Caesar's friend," which the Johannine Christians would see as descriptive of not only what happened to Jesus but what was happening in their own times if some Jews pressed for the Roman magistrates to prosecute Christians. (See the scenes described in Acts 13:50; 14:2; 17:5-8; 18:12.)

Similar animosity is found in Matthew 28:12-15, where a lie that the disciples stole the body of Jesus, started through a bribe given by the chief priests and elders, "has been spread among Jews until this day." One may guess that on the other side, among some Jews, a parallel was drawn between "that fellow" who caused trouble forty or fifty years ago and the present troublemakers who were making blasphemous claims about him.

If at this stage we can finally speak of anti-Judaism, notice that it took time to develop: It was not intrinsic to the Passion itself. This anti-Judaism reflects the unfriendly relationship between Christians (ethnically Jew or Gentile) and Jews who did not believe in Jesus.

Sometimes today there is pressure to drop from the New Testament as anti-Semitic such references to "the Jews." Nevertheless, I, for one, would resist strongly such a movement. Rather than seeking to "improve" the Passion narratives by eliminating such passages, those who preach or teach the Bible should wrestle honestly with how first-century conditions qualify and color what is reported. The final authors had in fact become antagonistic to Jews who did not believe in Jesus. We have no need to approve that hostility, but to excise such references is to censor what they intended.

Moreover, removing offensive passages enables hearers to accept unthinkingly everything they find in the Bible, whereas taking the trouble to explain the troublesome passages can lead to nuanced interpretation of the Bible and help to develop a mature rather than a simplistic understanding of the religious meaning of the Lord's Passion for today.

Stage Four was only the beginning of a long history; by the next century Christians would be accusing Jews of deicide

("God-killing"), and some Jewish legends would portray
Jesus as a wicked magician and the illegitimate son of an
adulteress. When the emperor Constantine became Christian
in the early fourth century and Christians began to gain
political power, the effect of the hostile feelings became one-
sided. This was the beginning of a tragic history that would
see the oppression and persecution of Jews continue through
the centuries, culminating horrendously in the Holocaust.

Many non-Christian elements contributed to that history,
particularly in the Nazi period. But often the Passion
narratives were read in a way that fueled hatred of Jews.

Hope for the Future

Careful biblical research may help efforts to ensure that
this never happens again. The recognition that important
Jewish figures in Jerusalem were hostile to Jesus and had a
role in his death need not of itself have produced anti-
Judaism, any more than the fact that the Jerusalem priests and
prophets plotted Jeremiah's death would produce such a
result.

The first Christian attempt to see theological significance in
Jesus' death by use of the scriptural portrayal of the just
persecuted by the wicked did not of itself have an anti-Jewish
tone. Anti-Judaism appeared when the death was interpreted
during times of bad relations between believers in Jesus (often
no longer ethnically Jewish) and Jews who did not believe in
him. Then it stuck.

Good relations between Christians and Jews based on
respect for each other will help us to read the Passion
narratives without an anti-Jewish effect. Without changing the
biblical text, Christians who appreciate the great heritage of
Judaism will work sensitively to correct the simplification
whereby those hostile to Jesus are portrayed without
qualification as "the Jews."

We Christians cannot dismiss or deny what happened to
Jesus. That would be the easy way out. It would be wrong. In
liturgically celebrating the truth and power of the Passion

narratives, however, we must be equally energetic in proclaiming, as did Pope John Paul II in 1995 during the fiftieth anniversary of the liberation of the Auschwitz Nazi death camp: "Never again anti-Semitism!"

CHAPTER SEVEN

The Easter Season: The Resurrection Narratives

The Resurrection of Christ is at the center of our faith. Paul affirms: "If Christ has not been raised, then our preaching is in vain, and your faith is in vain" (1 Corinthians 15:14). The Church devotes eight days of worship to retelling the Resurrection narratives. From Easter Sunday to the following (Low) Sunday the readings at Masses present one by one the many New Testament accounts of the appearances of the risen Lord.

Our four Gospels, written thirty to seventy years after the Resurrection, tell us what happened in different ways—so different that the Church wisely does not combine them all into one picture or prefer one Gospel account over the other. Each Gospel narrative should be allowed to contribute its own wealth to what we know and believe about the risen Christ.

How were these stories formed? Why do they differ from each other? What can we learn from their diversity? In this chapter we shall consider those questions. We should recognize that the Gospel accounts tell us what happened, enriched by insights acquired only after the early Christians looked back and put a whole series of events together.

Stories Told It Best

Our Christian ancestors spoke about the Resurrection long before they wrote about it. The first believers proclaimed the truth by word of mouth in forceful slogans and exclamations:

"The Lord was raised indeed, and has appeared to Simon [Peter]" (Luke 24:34). In Jerusalem in particular, biting challenges associate the crucifixion and the resurrection: "You crucified this Jesus...but God raised him up" (Acts 2:23-24; 4:10; 5:30-31; 10:39-40).

Four steps are mentioned by Paul in a formula delivered to him from the earliest days of his coming to faith: "That Christ died...that he was buried, that he was raised on the third day according to the Scriptures, and that he appeared..." (1 Corinthians 15:3-5). What this sequence of events meant for Jews and Gentiles alike is explained by Paul: Jesus was "put to death for our trespasses and raised for our justification" (Romans 4:25).

As vivid as these proclamations were, the story form proved to be a more effective way of conveying the full impact of the Resurrection. The association between the crucifixion and the resurrection needed to be fleshed out in a dramatic way so that those who were not present in Jerusalem could understand what God had done in making Jesus victorious over death. Consequently, the Gospel stories are quite different from the brief formulas preserved for us from the early preaching.

These brief, spoken formulas never mentioned the finding of Jesus' empty tomb. Yet in all four Gospels the empty tomb becomes the important link between the crucifixion and the resurrection—spotlighted as the site of the revelation that Jesus has conquered death. His followers saw his body placed in the tomb before the sabbath began; but when the sabbath was over, his body was no longer there. What happened?

Christians recognized that in itself the absence of the body did not prove divine intervention. At the moment of discovering the opened tomb, John 20:2 has Mary Magdalene conclude: "They"—presumably Jesus' enemies—"have taken the Lord from the tomb, and we do not know where they put him." But to their amazement the followers of Jesus learned that no such human explanation sufficed. The Jesus who had died appeared to them alive!

The appearances of the risen Jesus led Christians to a faith that enabled them to look back and see that the empty tomb itself already could be understood as a revelation that Jesus was no longer dead. The Gospel stories express that insight in a classical biblical manner. In the Old Testament at many significant moments God's communication is phrased by "an angel of the Lord"—a manifestation of God's presence in human form, constituting a bridge between heaven and earth. Such angels know God's plan and translate it into our language.

Accordingly, in all four Gospels an angel or angels appear at the tomb to make the meaning of the empty tomb crystal clear. The Gospels vary in their descriptions of the angel(s), whether there are one or two, and whether they are outside or inside the tomb, sitting or standing. These are the variations to be expected in a story transmitted orally. But the basic message of the angels is the same: *Jesus is no longer in the tomb because he has been raised!*

The empty tomb and the appearances of Jesus, then, are the two basic components of the Gospel narratives. They are reported in such a way that each casts light on the other to give a fuller understanding of the Resurrection. The preaching formulas, such as "The Lord is raised" or "God raised him up," did not explain how Jesus was victorious over death. Was the risen Jesus physical? Was he raised bodily? Paul argues that what is raised is not "physical" (*psychikos*) but "a spiritual body" (1 Corinthians 15:44). How is that subtle notion conveyed in narrative?

Once the angelic message explains why the tomb is empty, the tomb tells us that Jesus was raised in such a way that his body did not corrupt. In Jerusalem even those who refused to believe in Jesus never claimed they could point out his remains or skeleton in a burial place.

From another aspect, the way in which the appearances are described tells us that the Resurrection was *no mere resuscitation* of Jesus to ordinary life. When the risen Jesus appeared, he was not easily recognizable even to those who knew him well (for example, Mary Magdalene and Simon Peter). He could pass through locked doors; cover distances instantaneously; and yet he still pointed to his body as real. Thus there is no evidence whatsoever that early preaching ever involved anything other than *a bodily resurrection that involved tremendous transformation.*

According to the ancient tradition in 1 Corinthians 15:5-7, Jesus appeared to Cephas (Simon Peter; see Luke 24:34), to the Twelve, to more than five hundred, to James and all the apostles. Paul adds that Jesus appeared "last of all to me" (15:8).

There can be little doubt, then, that the preached tradition included a number of appearances; yet these were past and continued no longer. Where and when did they occur? What took place during them? And when did they stop? None of that is specified. The Gospel stories answer those questions, but the answers sometimes vary.

Here we encounter most clearly the pastoral genius of the evangelists. Each was addressing a different audience, and in recounting Jesus' public ministry each had emphasized aspects that spoke to the need of that special audience. Accordingly, each evangelist draws something from the tradition of the appearances of the risen Jesus that ties in clearly with what has been recounted in the body of his Gospel. Thus the readers (or hearers) of the Gospel could see how the Resurrection fitted consistently into the whole portrayal of Jesus. Very briefly let us look at the Gospels one by one, treating them in the probable order in which they were written.

Mark's Narrative(s)

Most scholars recognize that Mark's original ending consisted of 16:1-8. Because of the brief, almost unfinished character of that account, however, early Christians added other endings. The best known of these is 16:9-20 (found in all Catholic Bibles). Thus we may speak of two "Marcan" accounts of the Resurrection.

Mark 16:1-8, which is basically the story of the empty tomb, contains the heavenly revelation that Jesus is risen and promises his appearance in Galilee to the other disciples and Peter. Yet that appearance is never described, and the story ends with the women leaving the tomb afraid and silent.

Only through suffering will the disciples reach fuller understanding. Throughout the Gospel Mark emphasizes how difficult it was for those who followed Jesus to believe in him fully because they did not understand that suffering and rejection were an essential part of the identity of God's Son. In the great trial of Jesus' passion the male disciples have all failed and run away—an experience reflecting fear and shameful weakness. But their pain leads to light. After they have suffered and failed Jesus will appear to them in Galilee (Mark 14:27-28).

The women followers of Jesus, spared the Gethsemane trial where the disciples first fell asleep and then fled, looked on from a distance at the crucifixion. They too must experience the difficulty of faith; for even after they are told of the Resurrection, they do not automatically become proclaimers of Jesus' victory. Rather they flee in silence and fear (Mark 16:8).

That is not a bad warning for Christians today. Our faith has come to us from others who have passed on to us the revelation of what God has done, but the fact that we have accepted that proclamation does not mean that we have full Christian faith. Even after the Resurrection we may have to carry the cross and experience suffering and rejection before we reach a real understanding of the Jesus in whom we say we believe.

Faith comes from a personal understanding of the risen Lord. Of course Mark does not mean that the women were permanently silent and afraid. The added ending (Mark 16:9-20) recognizes that point by showing how, not only for the women but also for other followers, an encounter with the risen Jesus brought about faith. In each case that personal encounter accomplished what a message received from others could not.

We also hear how those whom Jesus upbraids for lack of faith and hardness of heart are entrusted with preaching the gospel to the whole world. These are messages pertinent to our own lives. No amount of hearing about Jesus ever substitutes for a personal experience of him, and neither then nor now was the task of bringing others to Christ entrusted only to the saintly perfect. Mark's Gospel reminds us that Jesus' first disciples were struggling human beings like ourselves.

Matthew's Narrative

As always, Matthew, although he draws on Mark, is the more skilled teacher, kinder to readers who do not always see implications. Mark 16:1-8 does not actually describe appearances of the risen Jesus, but Matthew does. Thus in 28:9 he tells of an appearance to the women after they left the tomb—an appearance (echoed in John and Mark 16:9) that may well represent ancient tradition even though it was never part of the official preaching (such as reported by Paul in 1 Corinthians 15).

Some people attempt to block the resurrection of Jesus. Even more dramatically, in Matthew 27:62-66; 28:4, 11-15 we are told of a scheme to frustrate the Resurrection by getting Pilate's soldiers to guard Jesus' tomb. One of the tragic elements in Matthew's Christian experience is a hostile relationship between synagogue authorities and Christian believers. That is reflected from start to finish in Matthew's Gospel.

At the very beginning of his Gospel, Matthew portrayed King Herod, the chief priests and the scribes plotting to destroy the newly born Messiah (2:3-5, 16-18, 20); but God frustrated them. Now, at the end of the Gospel, Matthew portrays the prefect Pilate, the chief priests and the Pharisees plotting against Jesus. Once more God intervenes to frustrate them. Though the polemic attitude behind this story should not be imitated, Matthew reminds us that the Christian proclamation of the gospel will not be without struggle.

Jesus in Galilee promises to be "with us" always. Last of all, Matthew describes what Mark only promised: the appearance of Jesus to the (Eleven) disciples in Galilee. In the opening of the public ministry in Galilee (Matthew 5—7) Jesus delivered on a mountain a "sermon" that contained the essentials of his new teaching about the Kingdom of God. In 10:6-7 Jesus sent his disciples to preach that Kingdom "to the lost sheep of the house of Israel." Now from a mountain in Galilee the risen Jesus sends his disciples forth to teach "all nations," making them disciples by baptizing them.

Matthew's community has seen this shift from Jews to Gentiles as the focus of the ministry. Yet Matthew is careful to show that God's plan for Jesus was consistent from beginning to end. The revelation given about Jesus before he was born (1:23) proclaimed that he would be Emmanuel ("God with us"); Jesus' last words are "I am with you all days to the end of time" (28:20).

Luke's Narrative

Like Matthew, Luke follows Mark in the basic story of the empty tomb, but then goes his own way in the appearances he reports. While Matthew recounts an appearance of Jesus in Jerusalem to two women, Luke recounts at length (24:13-35) the appearance of Jesus to two male disciples on the road from Jerusalem to Emmaus. In the Acts of the Apostles (2:42, 46; 20:7, 11), which Luke also authored as a sequel to his Gospel account, he points to the role of "the breaking of the bread" in Christian community life. He prepares for that in the Emmaus story by having the disciples recognize Jesus in the breaking of the bread.

This is still an important theme for our life as believers today since the eucharistic breaking of the bread constitutes one of our principal ways of encountering the presence of the risen Jesus—a unique presence different from all others.

Luke sees the Resurrection as fulfilling the Scriptures. Next Luke turns to the appearance of the risen Jesus to the Eleven. More than either Mark or Matthew, Luke stresses what was already implicit in the empty tomb: the reality of the body of the risen Jesus, who was not simply a spirit (24:37-43).

Particularly significant is that the risen Jesus teaches the Eleven about his death and resurrection by explaining the Scriptures, "All the things written about me in the Law of Moses, and in the prophets and in the psalms must be fulfilled" (24:44).

Already the two disciples on the road to Emmaus found their hearts burning when he opened to them the Scriptures, but now this has become a major theme. Once again Luke's emphasis is preparing the way for the Church life he will describe in his Acts of the Apostles, where Peter, Stephen and Paul begin their preaching by emphasizing that the Scriptures anticipate what happened to Jesus (Acts 2:14-21; 7:1-50; 13:16-22).

Luke spotlights Jerusalem as the setting for Jesus' appearances and ascension. Matthew places the appearance of the risen Jesus to the Eleven in Galilee. For Matthew's purposes, this region was a fitting selection from the tradition, since Galilee is the land of the Gentiles (4:15) and Jesus after his Resurrection instructs his disciples to go and make disciples of the Gentiles (28:19). Luke places the appearance to the Eleven in Jerusalem. This was a fitting selection from the tradition for Luke's purposes. For him the Gospel began with the appearance of Gabriel to Zechariah in the Jerusalem temple; now it ends with Jesus' disciples in the temple blessing God.

Most of us are familiar with the imagery at the beginning of Acts (1:3, 9-12) where Jesus ascends into heaven from the Mount of Olives forty days after the Resurrection. Yet at the very end of his Gospel (24:50-51), Luke has him ascend into heaven from the same region on Easter Sunday night.

In this "double exposure" we see Luke's theological perceptivity. In one sense (dramatically portrayed in the Gospel) *Jesus' return to God was the end of his earthly career*, a career beginning and ending in Jerusalem and thus symbolically lived within the confines of Judaism. In another sense (dramatically portrayed in Acts) *Jesus' return to God begins the life of the Church* that starts in Jerusalem (Judaism) and extends to Rome (the Gentile world).

John's Narrative

The account in John 20, like Mark 16:9-20 and Luke, has the appearances of Jesus in Jerusalem. The account in John 21 (which is only superficially connected to John 20), like Matthew and Mark 16:7, has the appearance of Jesus in Galilee. Both Chapters 20 and 21 are appropriate to John's thought, but each in a different way.

John's Gospel narrates a series of encounters as character after character comes to meet Jesus in center stage and reacts to him. This atmosphere continues in John 20 where sequentially Peter and the Beloved Disciple, Mary Magdalene, the disciples and Thomas encounter the mystery of Jesus' Resurrection.

The Beloved Disciple is the first to believe. In the tradition (1 Corinthians 15:5; Luke 24:34), Simon Peter was the first among the male disciples of Jesus to see the risen Jesus. John does not violate that but still exemplifies his peculiar emphasis: Throughout the latter part of the Gospel the unnamed Beloved Disciple, the one particularly loved by Jesus, is closer than Peter to the master. In John 20:3-10, where Peter and the Beloved Disciple go to the tomb, neither sees Jesus; but the Beloved Disciple comes to faith without an appearance of the risen One.

Mary Magdalene is the first to proclaim the risen Lord. As in Matthew and the added ending of Mark, Mary Magdalene is the first follower to see the risen Jesus. Here she does not recognize him by sight but does when he calls her name, fulfilling the Good Shepherd's prediction that he will call by name the sheep that belong to him and they will follow him (John 10:3-5). Jesus speaks to her of "my Father and your Father" and refers to his disciples as his "brothers." Thus, to Magdalene Jesus fulfills the promise in John's Prologue (1:12): "All those who did accept him he empowered to be God's children." If the Beloved Disciple was the first to believe, Mary becomes the first to proclaim the risen Lord.

Jesus' disciples are recreated by the Holy Spirit. Next (20:19-23), Jesus appears to the group of disciples, consisting of or including members of the Twelve. Just as in Genesis 2:7 the Lord God formed a human being out of the dust of the earth by breathing into the nostrils the breath of life, so Jesus breathes on the disciples and they receive the Holy Spirit, recreating them as God's children with eternal life. For them this is the birth of the Spirit promised in John 3:5. Throughout the Gospel Jesus has referred to himself as the one sent by God; the disciples are now sent to continue his work in the world with his power over evil and sin.

Thomas the doubter. The various Gospels mention doubt when Jesus appears to his followers after the Resurrection (Matthew 28:17; Luke 24:37-38; Mark 16:14), but in 20:24-29 John dramatizes that doubt in an individual. Paradoxically, however, from the lips of this "doubting Thomas" comes the highest confession of faith in all the Gospels: "My Lord and my God." The Gospel began with the Prologue's affirmation (1:1), "The Word was God." Now human beings have come to recognize that.

Peter as missionary and pastor. John 21 moves the setting to Galilee and highlights two scenes related to Simon Peter's career. A miraculous catch of fish directed by the risen Jesus is dragged ashore by Peter, a symbol of the missionary role he will have. But then the symbolism shifts abruptly as Peter is commissioned to feed Jesus' sheep.

The shift reflects Christian experience: A great missionary thrust in the first generations eventually ceded to pastoral care for those brought to Christ. John's stress on Jesus as the unique "Good Shepherd" has slowed the acceptance of human shepherds in the Johannine community; but when a shepherding role is authenticated through the symbolism of Peter, very Johannine conditions are attached. Peter must love Jesus and the sheep do not become his—they still belong to Jesus.

The final focus on the Beloved Disciple. The last word of Jesus, however, is not about Peter but about the Beloved Disciple. He is given no role of authority, but he retains a primacy in being loved, which is more important in this Gospel. To this disciple is held open the possibility of being there when Jesus returns. Symbolically that would be the final fruit of the Resurrection: a believing community of Christian disciples that would remain until the last days.

Diverse Messages

We come back to the important pastoral question with which we began: What can we learn from the fact that the Gospel accounts of the Resurrection differ from each other? The answer is centered in the risen Jesus as God's ultimate revelation directed to all times and places. The evangelists shaped the Resurrection narratives to be meaningful to audiences of differing life-styles and backgrounds in the first century.

Jesus Christ is the same, yesterday, today and forever; but the world addressed by God's revelation in Christ is varied indeed. The Church of our century cannot present a different Christ. But by the way it preserves the varied Gospel messages, it lets Jesus speak to the differing needs of the audiences of our times.

CHAPTER EIGHT

The Fundamentalist Challenge: A Catholic Response

A questioner once asked me: Is it so bad that a Catholic becomes a biblical fundamentalist? Wouldn't a fundamentalist still believe in many basic doctrines of the Christian faith and have a solid moral code? The answer is yes; but biblical fundamentalism, despite what it can preserve, really distorts the challenge of Jesus Christ. It provides an absolute certainty based on a belief that every word in the Bible really has been dictated by God and one needs only hold to the literal meaning. It does not recognize that every word in the Bible, even though inspired by God, has been written by human beings who had limitations.

The message of the Incarnation is that there is no way to avoid the interplay of the divine and the human in approaching God. Biblical literalism, since it makes all divine, supplies a false certitude that often unconsciously confuses the human limitation with the divine message. A literalist interpretation destroys the very nature of the Bible as a human expression of divine revelation.

One must understand that only human beings speak words. Therefore the valid description of the Bible as "God's word" has both the divine element ("God's") and the human ("word").

Some 'Don'ts' and 'Do's'

Those familiar with what works and what doesn't work in responding to fundamentalist challenges have come up with the following bits of wisdom.

Don't waste time arguing over individual biblical texts with fundamentalists. The question is much larger—an overall view of religion, of Christianity and of the nature of the Bible.

Don't attack fundamentalists as if they were fools. Often biblical literalism is an attitude of self-defense even on the part of extremely intelligent people. They want to preserve their faith in God, and this seems to them the only way. They will understand your attacks on them as an attack on their faith. Indeed, were you to be successful in convincing an intelligent biblical fundamentalist that the position is wrong, you might be surprised to find that the former fundamentalist does not become a more moderate Christian but an atheist.

Some fundamentalists are very well informed about biblical technicalities, such as languages. Occasionally, evangelists know a lot more about the Bible than the average Catholic priest or mainline Protestant minister.

Don't be sure that your standard arguments against fundamentalism will work. Biblical fundamentalists have developed careful defenses against the contrary arguments that they have encountered. For instance, if you triumphantly point to the fossil argument supporting evolution, you may be surprised to find a fundamentalist who maintains that God created the world with fossils already in it and that therefore such fossils tell us nothing about the antiquity of the world.

An important "do" is to present the Bible in an intelligent, nonliteralist way. There is no use moaning about the number of fundamentalist media preachers if we have no one in the media presenting the Bible in a sensible, nonliteral manner based on modern biblical approaches, and not simply using the text as a jumping-off point for a pietistic homily. When fundamentalists are the only ones to offer people knowledge about the Bible, people will go to fundamentalists. A solid, scholarly approach to the Bible can be spiritually nourishing and mentally satisfying. Catholics must encourage that in the media.

One might object that on the Catholic scene there is a shortage of priests and that some priests are not good expositors of the Bible. Then one must capitalize on the real interest among the laity, who should be tapped and professionally prepared for this service. If as a Church we recognize this as a major problem, we should mobilize our forces in order to supply intelligent biblical leadership among Catholics.

Effective teaching of the Bible is not a challenge that affects Roman Catholics alone, and so there is no reason why mainline Protestant Churches and Catholics cannot join in a common effort to present the Bible intelligently in the media. Some other Churches have developed excellent textbooks for reading the Bible.

The fear of losing Roman Catholic doctrine if we cooperate with other Churches in such biblical exposition is largely exaggerated. Indeed, if such cooperation were sponsored by various Church leaders, I think they would all recognize that the essential issue is to communicate a basic, intelligent approach to the Bible. It would respect Christian doctrine on which we all agree.

Ten Challenges and Responses

Often Roman Catholics become a bit tongue-tied when the teachings of their faith are challenged by biblical fundamentalists. Many Roman Catholics are very articulate in explaining the doctrines of their faith—the Mass, the sacraments, the papacy, Mary and the saints—in the words and phrases remembered from their catechism. But nothing in their training equips them to handle the objections that such beliefs are *nonbiblical*. Their first reaction to a fundamentalist probing may be to respond in terms of Church teaching—a response that confirms the fundamentalist in the opinion that Catholic beliefs are totally foreign to the Bible. It might help if

Catholics were able to speak about these issues in biblical language that fundamentalists might understand.

Consequently, I offer here ten responses to ten challenges often raised by fundamentalists against Catholic positions. I have tried to formulate these responses so that they present the Catholic positions *in terms of biblical faith*.

Obviously, there may be more than one way to phrase the Catholic responses from a biblical perspective. I think my wordings, which I have tested on friends, are accurate, but I don't pretend that they exhaust the full meaning of Catholic faith on the subjects discussed. I am treating only aspects of those subjects that are of most concern to biblical fundamentalists.

I have tried to put the challenges in everyday language— just the way you might hear them in a conversation with a Christian fundamentalist at your front door or during a lunch break at work. The challenges are in the form of questions reflecting how fundamentalists understand Catholic positions that bother them.

1) Why don't Catholics see the Scriptures as containing the fullness of God's revelation instead of always running to the teaching authority of the Catholic Church for God's truth?

The Roman Catholic Church considers itself a biblical Church in the sense that it acknowledges and proclaims the Bible to be God's word. In the teachings of Moses and the prophets, and in the teachings of Jesus proclaimed by the apostles, to which the Scriptures bear witness, the Catholic Church acknowledges a unique self-revelation by God to humankind. The Church confesses the sufficiency of the revelation witnessed by the Bible in the sense that neither a new revealer nor new special revelations are necessary for men and women to find the will of God and the grace of salvation.

If great attention has been given to the teaching of the ongoing Church in Roman Catholicism, that teaching is not presented in terms of a new revelation but as the result of the

Church's continuing task to proclaim the biblical revelation in light of new problems in new generations. In carrying on that task, the Church regards itself as the instrument of the promised Paraclete-Spirit who would take what Jesus had given and guide Christians along the way of truth in subsequent times (John 16:13).

2) *The Bible teaches us that we are saved through faith in Jesus Christ, our sole mediator. Why do Catholics contradict this by teaching that people can be saved through good works or by praying to the saints?*

The Catholic Church proclaims to its people that, just as the Bible indicates, justification and redemption come through the grace given by God because of the death and resurrection of Jesus. Human beings cannot earn redemption or salvation. Neither is it won through good works. Good works are done through God's grace in response to God's redemptive work in Christ. Accordingly, Christ is the unique mediator between God and human beings.

Roman Catholicism has recognized the intercession of the saints. That is part of its understanding of the biblical injunction that we must pray for one another. The "we" includes not only believers on earth, but those who have gone before us as saints in God's presence in heaven. Such intercession is useful and salutary but in no way necessary in the sense in which the mediation of Jesus Christ is necessary. Any intercession on the part of the saints must be accepted by God and joined to the supreme intercession of the one high priest, Jesus Christ. There is no other name by which we may be saved, as Acts 4:12 affirms.

3) *Why don't Catholics recognize we are saved through a personal relationship to Jesus Christ, not through membership in a Church?*

While the Catholic Church proclaims the all-sufficiency of the redemptive death and resurrection of Jesus Christ, it acknowledges that Christians must respond in faith and commitment to Christ so that God's redemptive grace may transform them as children of God. Therefore, encountering Christ and believing in him in a personal way is very much a part of Roman Catholic thought.

Jesus Christ redeemed a people—that is why we belong to a Church—and one becomes part of that people by adhesion to Christ.

Baptism of infants, which makes them part of the Christian family of God, in no way is meant to substitute for the later personal decision that is intrinsically a Christian demand. As people grow up, Baptism and personal commitment must accompany each other in the wholeness of Christian faith.

4) Why do Catholic priests repeat what you call "the Sacrifice of the Mass" instead of recognizing that Christ died once and for all and that his death can be the only Christian sacrifice?

Following the New Testament injunction of Jesus, "Do this in memory of me," the Catholic Church in its liturgy regularly breaks the bread that is the Body of Christ and offers the cup that is the communion in his Blood. It accepts fully the teaching of the Epistle to the Hebrews that the sacrifice of Jesus Christ on the cross is once and for all. There is no need for other sacrifices.

The liturgy of the Last Supper, which we call the Mass, is a sacrifice in the sense that it makes present again to Christians of different times and places the possibility of participating in the Body and Blood of Christ in commemoration of him, proclaiming the death of the Lord until he comes. The Mass is in no way a separate sacrifice from the sacrifice of the cross. It is not a new sacrifice replacing the sacrifice of the cross or adding to it as if that sacrifice were insufficient. Jesus, the Catholic Church holds, is the one high priest of the new covenant.

Catholics refer to our clergy as priests. That terminology recognizes that when a Christian designated by ordination presides at the Eucharist, which recalls the death of the Lord until he comes, that person represents Jesus the high priest and not merely the community. Our doctrine of the Mass as representing the one priestly sacrifice of Jesus is, in our judgment, fully biblical.

5) Why do Catholics go to the Church and its sacraments as the source of grace rather than to the Savior himself?

Christ saves Christians in and through the Church. The Church, which is the Body of Christ for which he gave himself (Ephesians 5:23, 25), has great dignity and importance; but the Church itself does not save people. We believe that Christ is operative in the sacraments of the Church and that it is Christ who gives the grace that touches lives. The Catholic teaching that the sacraments work *ex opere operato* (that is, grace is conferred through the sacramental action) never should be understood to mean that the sacrament of itself, independently of Christ, is effective. That formula guarantees that the efficacy of the sacraments is not dependent on the administrator of the sacrament. Rather, for those who are disposed to receive his grace, Christ is operative in the sacrament.

6) Why do Catholics say that the pope is the head of the Church when Scripture says that Christ is the head?

Catholics believe that Jesus Christ is the head of the Body, the Church. No human can take his place, dispensing with his headship. The pope has no authority independent of Christ or in rivalry with him. Even as the New Testament speaks of overseers or bishops guiding individual Churches, the pope is an overseer through whom Christ supplies guidance to the whole Church, keeping it in the truth of the gospel.

7) Why do Catholics look on Mary as divine or more-than-human instead of recognizing that she needed salvation?

In Catholic faith Mary, like all other descendants of Adam, had to be redeemed through Christ. We honor her especially for two biblical reasons: (1) She is the mother of Jesus, who is Lord and God. (2) According to Luke 1:26-38, she is the first to hear the good news of Jesus' identity and to say, "Be it done to me according to your word"—thus becoming the first disciple to meet Jesus' standard of hearing the word of God and doing it (see Luke 8:21).

We believe that God gave her special privileges, but these are related to the graces of discipleship given through Christ and in no way divinize her. All believers in Christ are delivered by his grace from the sin of Adam; all believers in Christ will be raised bodily from the dead. Catholics believe that Mary, the first one to profess belief in Christ as revealed by an angel, was through Christ's grace the first to be totally freed from Adam's sin (conceived without sin) and the first to be raised bodily (assumed into heaven).

While we acknowledge that these doctrines of the Immaculate Conception and Assumption of Mary are not found in the New Testament, we hold them as consonant with the picture in Luke of Mary as the first one to believe, and with the picture in John where she is especially honored as Jesus hangs on the cross. The doctrines preserve insights faithful to a direction supplied by Scripture.

8) Why do Catholics neglect the biblical teaching that Christ is coming back again?

We Catholics believe in the second coming of Christ. For us that means that God has yet to establish fully the Kingdom and to judge the world. All this will be accomplished through Christ and is not attainable by human endeavor. As for when, through the coming of Christ, God will establish the Kingdom, we believe in the teaching of Jesus recorded in Acts 1:7: "It is not for you to know the times or seasons which the Father has fixed by his own authority." All human guesses as to the time of the second coming must yield to that biblical teaching.

9) Why does the Catholic Church discourage private interpretation of Scripture and make its members submit to official teaching?

We Catholics do not exaggerate the principle that the Church is the interpreter of Scripture. The Roman Catholic Church has rarely, if ever, defined what a text meant to the person who wrote it. The Church encourages interpreters of Scripture to discover with all the means available to them what individual passages meant when they were written and encourages all of its members to read the Bible for spiritual nourishment.

Church interpretation for Catholics deals primarily not with what the biblical text meant when it was written, but with what it means for the life of the Christian community in subsequent eras. On essential issues the Spirit who inspired the Scriptures will not allow the whole community of believers to be misled about faith and moral behavior.

Individuals reading from their Bible may come to radical conclusions. This has indeed happened in the course of history. Some have even denied the divinity of Christ, the Resurrection, creation by God and the Ten Commandments. The Catholic Church will take its guidance on such biblical matters from the long tradition of Christian teaching stemming from reflecting on the Bible.

10) Why don't Catholics defend God's word in the Bible against all possibility of error, scientific matters included?

The Roman Catholic Church teaches that the Bible communicates without error that truth which God intended for the sake of our salvation. Affirming biblical inerrancy (freedom from error) in that sense, it also resists modern attempts to make the Bible answer problems that the biblical authors never thought of. It resists attempts to take biblical texts that envisioned other situations and apply them without qualification to situations of our times. Some of the conflicts between Roman Catholic practices and "literal" interpretations of the Bible rest precisely on this point.

The Roman Catholic Church believes that none of its positions are in conflict with the literal interpretation of the Scriptures, when "literal" means *what the author intended in his times as a communication of the truth that God wanted for the sake of our salvation.* It resists the use of biblical interpretation to support scientific or historical statements that lay beyond the competency of the biblical authors in their times.

'The Historical Truth of the Gospels'— *Instruction* of the Roman Pontifical Biblical Commission (1964)

Prefatory Remarks

As explained in Chapter One above, the occasion for this *Instruction* was the defeat of a very conservative preliminary document on *The Sources of Divine Revelation* submitted to the Second Vatican Council in late 1962. That *schema* had been drawn up by forces in Rome hoping to repeal the biblical reforms of Pope Pius XII. After its defeat, a new drafting committee was commissioned. Their work was considerably facilitated by the issuance of this *Instruction* by the Biblical Commission with the approval of Pope Paul VI. It is a long document, and I quote here only from the sections (VI-X) pertaining to the formation of the Gospels.

These sections correspond to the majority view of centrist scholars, Protestant as well as Catholic, about Gospel origins. (For the translation of the whole and a commentary by J. A. Fitzmyer, who himself has served on the Biblical Commission, see *Theological Studies* 25 [1964], pages 386-408, from which translation I have adapted below.) To facilitate finding one's way in my own discussion (see Chapter Two), I have added headings in italics and italicized certain key affirmations.

The Text of the *Instruction*

VI, 2: To judge properly concerning the reliability of what is transmitted in the Gospels, the interpreter should pay diligent attention to the three stages of tradition by which the doctrine and the life of Jesus have come down to us.

Stage One: The Ministry of Jesus. VII: Christ our Lord joined to himself chosen disciples who followed him from the beginning, saw his deeds, heard his words, and in this way were equipped to be witnesses of his life and doctrine. When the Lord was orally explaining his doctrine, *he followed the modes of reasoning and exposition that were in vogue at the time. He accommodated himself to the mentality of his listeners* and saw to it that what he taught was firmly impressed on the mind and easily remembered by the disciples. These men understood the miracles and other events of the life of Jesus correctly: as deeds performed or designed that people might believe in Christ through them, and embrace with faith the doctrine of salvation.

Stage Two: The Preaching of the Apostles. VIII: The apostles proclaimed above all the death and resurrection of the Lord, as they bore witness to Jesus. They faithfully explained his life and words, while taking into account in their method of preaching the circumstances in which their listeners found themselves. *After Jesus rose from the dead and his divinity was clearly perceived*, faith, far from destroying the memory of what had transpired, rather confirmed it, because their faith rested on the things that Jesus did and taught. Nor was he changed into a "mythical" person and his teaching deformed in consequence of the worship that the disciples from that time on paid Jesus as the Lord and the Son of God. On the other hand there is no reason to deny that *the apostles passed on to their listeners what was really said and done by the Lord with that fuller understanding that they enjoyed*, having been instructed by the glorious events of the Christ and taught by the light of the Spirit of Truth. And so, just as Jesus himself after his resurrection "interpreted to them" the words of the Old Testament as well as his own, *they too interpreted his*

words and deeds according to the needs of their listeners.
"Devoting themselves to the ministry of the word," they
preached and made use of various modes of speaking that
were suited to their own purpose and the mentality of their
listeners. For they were debtors "to Greeks and barbarians, to
the wise and foolish." But these modes of speaking with
which the preachers proclaimed Christ must be distinguished
and (properly) assessed: catecheses, stories, testimonia,
hymns, doxologies, prayers—and other *literary forms* of this
sort which were in Sacred Scripture and accustomed to be
used by people of that time.

Stage Three: The Writing by the Evangelists. IX: This
primitive instruction, which was at first passed on by word of
mouth and then in writing—for it soon happened that many
tried "to compile a narrative of things" that concerned the
Lord Jesus—was committed to writing by the sacred authors
in four Gospels for the benefit of the Churches, with a method
suited to the particular purpose which each (author) set for
himself. *From the many things handed down they selected some
things, reduced others to a synthesis, (still) others they explicated as
they kept in mind the situation of the Churches.* With every
(possible) means they sought that their readers might become
aware of the reliability of those words by which they had
been instructed. Indeed, from what they had received the
sacred writers above all selected the things that were suited to
the various situations of the faithful and to the purpose that
they had in mind, and adapted their narrative of them to the
same situations and purpose. Since the meaning of a
statement also depends on the sequence, the evangelists, in
passing on the words and deeds of our Savior, explained
these now in one context, now in another, depending on
(their) usefulness to the readers. Consequently, let the exegete
seek out the meaning intended by the evangelist in narrating
a saying or a deed in a certain way or in placing it in a certain
context. *For the truth of the story is not at all affected by the fact
that the evangelists relate the words and deeds of the Lord in a
different order, and express his sayings not literally but differently,
while preserving (their) sense.* For, as St. Augustine says, "It is

quite probable that each evangelist believed it to have been his duty to recount what he had to in that order in which it pleased God to suggest it to his memory—in those things at least in which the order, whether it be this or that, detracts in nothing from the truth and authority of the Gospel. But why the Holy Spirit, who apportions individually to each one as He wills, and who therefore undoubtedly also governed and ruled the minds of the holy (writers) in recalling what they were to write because of the preeminent authority that the books were to enjoy, permitted one to compile his narrative in this way and another in that, anyone with pious diligence may seek the reason and with divine aid will be able to find it."

X: Unless exegetes pay attention to all these things that pertain to the origin and composition of the Gospels and make proper use of all the laudable achievements of recent research, they will not fulfill their task of probing into what the sacred writers intended and what they really said. From the results of the new investigation it is apparent that *the doctrine and life of Jesus were not simply reported for the sole purpose of being remembered, but were "preached" so as to offer the Church a basis of faith and of morals.* The interpreter (then), by tirelessly scrutinizing the testimony of the evangelists, will be able to illustrate more profoundly the perennial theological value of the Gospels and bring out clearly how necessary and important the Church's interpretation is.